Decorating OLD HOUSE INTERIORS

30 Classic American Styles

Decorating OLD HOUSE INTERIORS

30 Classic American Styles

Written and Illustrated by
Lawrence Schwin III

Sterling Publishing Co., Inc.   New York
A STERLING/MAIN STREET BOOK

In loving memory of my father,
Lawrence Schwin, whose love, support,
integrity, and encouragement will
always remain with me.

And in grateful memory of my editor,
Larry Grow, who suggested this book
and encouraged me to undertake it.

Library of Congress Cataloging-in-Publication Data.

Schwin, Lawrence.
   Decorating old house interiors / written & illustrated by Lawrence
Schwin III.
      p.   cm.
   "A Sterling/Main Street book."
   Includes index.
   ISBN 0-8069-7431-1
   1. Interior decoration—United States—Themes, motives.
I. Title.
NK2002.S35 1994
747.213—dc20   93-49719
                                      CIP

Designed by Lawrence Schwin III
Additional graphic design by John Murphy
Typeset by Upper Case Limited, Cork, Ireland.

A Sterling/Main Street Book

10 9 8 7 6 5 4 3 2 1

First paperback edition published in 1996 by
Sterling Publishing Company, Inc.
387 Park Avenue South, New York, N.Y. 10016
© 1994 by Lawrence Schwin III
Distributed in Canada by Sterling Publishing
c/o Canadian Manda Group, One Atlantic Avenue, Suite 105
Toronto, Ontario, Canada M6K 3E7
Distributed in Great Britain and Europe by Cassell PLC
Wellington House, 125 Strand, London WC2R 0BB, England
Distributed in Australia by Capricorn Link (Australia) Pty Ltd.
P.O. Box 6651, Baulkham Hills, Business Centre, NSW 2153, Australia

Printed in Hong Kong
All rights reserved

Sterling ISBN 0-8069-7431-1 Trade
             0-8069-7434-6 Paper

Contents

Preface 7
Introduction 9

Preface

JUST ABOUT EVERYONE is interested in houses and interior decoration. Young children take special interest in their rooms and as young adults often take pains in creating dorm-room decor that characterizes their emerging individualism. Young couples spend much time and effort fixing-up their first homes and in personalizing bland apartments while looking ahead to their dream homes. For those in their golden years, rooms and surroundings are of special importance, and, though many may have been pared down for easier manageability, almost all represent a strong sense of their lives with families and feelings of familiarity and continuity which can be especially meaningful to scattered family members. Throughout American history, interiors have represented places of refuge, comfort, and security—especially in periods of settlement, when homesickness and a vast unknown wilderness were strong facts of daily life. Most Americans fortunate enough to have built or found houses in which to set down roots have found comfort in familiar and comfortable surroundings.

Interest in historic interiors has become widespread only since the middle of the twentieth century. Though once the almost exclusive province of the well-to-do, period rooms are now appreciated and studied by more people than ever before. The growth and development of the historic house museum and restored communities, together with our ability to travel to them easily, has been in large measure responsible for this widespread interest. In addition, the almost traumatic scientific and cultural changes of the final decades of the twentieth century have fostered, without question, a very real sense of nostalgia for a past that seems to retreat at an ever-increasing pace. Interest in our historic patrimony has also increased because of the loss of so much of the architectural fabric of our towns and cities. Everyone is familiar with communities where old and historically important structures have been replaced by formless, ugly buildings—commissioned and designed by people devoid of any understanding of scale, texture, context, and the needs and wants of human inhabitants. The resulting sense of existing "nowhere" brings to mind an axiom of the historic preservation movement: "Communities without old buildings and the sense of the past which they impart are like people without souls." Indeed, what hope is there for the future of our society if we no longer recognize our past?

Decorating Old House Interiors is intended for anyone who is interested in American interiors. I hope it will encourage as well many who have never taken a particular interest in the subject, and that this might be accomplished through the drawings and illustrations which represent my own consuming interest in old house interiors. While the book will provide ideas about period interior design for those with old houses, it is also intended to offer basic information towards the development of a deeper appreciation of the subject. One does not need to own a superb mid-eighteenth-century colonial to take inspiration from the stylistic trends of that period, nor does anyone have to buy a turreted Queen Anne mansion to profit aesthetically from the decorative objects of that era. In fact, contemporary structures can provide wonderful and striking backgrounds for period furniture and decorative accessories that often need only to be "pulled together" by accurate and authentic period textiles, wallpapers, carpets, and paint colors. Consequently, all of the textiles, wallpapers, carpets, and decorative objects illustrated in the pages that follow possess the timeless integrity and design qualities that are at home in any era, and especially in our own.

Within the book's thirty principal sections, both the character and the look of major decorative periods are presented through drawings, photographs, and actual samples of historic and reproduction textiles, wallpapers, and carpets. In several instances, representative pages from period books, and photographs of people from the periods under discussion, are also included. Interiors are considerably more than an assemblage of decorative objects and are, with very few exceptions, intended as environments in which people live and interact with one another.

Children's interpretations of houses by Lois and Larry Maples.

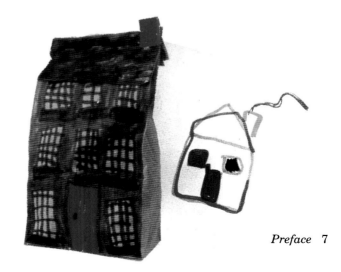

Each of the thirty major sections includes a perspective drawing of a building representative of the period discussed in order to provide an architectural context in which to place the section's featured interior which appears opposite it. All of the drawings—exterior and interior—are hypothetical, though based upon the decorative trends of the periods they represent. Following each of these two pages are two additional pages, providing many of the essential ingredients of each decorative period and encouraging study. Like the drawings, intended to bring the reader into the subject, the photographs and drawings on these pages are meant to defuse some of the fear about collecting that many of us have—particularly the belief that many decorative objects are only for museums and far beyond our reach. Dates assigned to each of the historic periods in this book are intended to approximate the period represented by the interior view. As in most interiors today, furnishings and objects from several periods were generally found in historic interiors—a fact difficult to illustrate in a book attempting to deal with some of the major interior trends of the past. All interior views shown are, with one exception, my own interpretations of historic interiors and do not represent or illustrate actual settings. The exception is the White House Oval Salon, c. 1809, in chapter 8.

Each of us is bound in our interpretations of the past by the period in which we live, the experiences we've had, and by our own ideas, likes, and dislikes—or that abstract thing called "taste." Most of us will be interested in creating a "period feeling" rather than creating a strict, historically accurate interior so carefully arranged that all modern conveniences are excluded, or at least carefully hidden. For those determined to create such interiors, it is best to keep in mind that not even the most gifted curator can reproduce a room setting exactly as it was at one given time in its past. We are all bound by the reality that just outside the windows is the present day; the past, in short, can never be truly re-created. Of course, if an historic interior is furnished with authentic period furnishings, the fact that the furniture was originally "modern"—that is, new and freshly stained or painted—is very often overlooked.

In addition to illustrating the major design elements of thirty historic periods, *Decorating Old House Interiors* encourages the reader to become involved in the design process itself and suggests step-by-step ways through which anyone can learn to take accurate field measurements, draw simple floor plans, construct interior models, and even make perspective drawings as tools towards planning an interior project. The book shows how re-creating the interiors of the historic past or drawing inspiration from them in contemporary applications is more complex than merely choosing an "early American" chair and a "colonial" textile from the local furniture store. With this information and the better understanding of period interiors it provides, the reader should be better able to create spaces imbued with the spirit of the past. In addition to information about the companies that reproduce historically accurate fabrics, wallpapers, and carpets, and whose work is shown throughout the book, there are several pages of full-color paint swatches which reference each of the thirty architectural periods and which can be easily matched by numerous paint companies across the county. (These colors, though close to the originals, are of course approximate and are limited only by the inability of even modern presses to reproduce fully accurate color in books.) Readers are also advised about working with professionals, both interior designers and architects, and presented with sources for further reading and study. The best study of all, of course, is to visit the many historic sites across America that have been accurately restored to re-create the living environments of the past.

Introduction

FEW PEOPLE living today can even begin to imagine what the earliest American colonists and settlers must have felt as they gazed from the windows of their houses into the vast, lonely, and mysterious pine-shrouded forests just a few feet from their doorsteps. To be sure there must have been a mixture of fear, respect, awe, and a goodly amount of homesickness in their minds, especially when they considered the heavy demands that colonial life placed on them. On the other hand, these men and women were people of strong faith, deep conviction, and rock-ribbed purpose with a good idea of the trials and hardships that faced them.

Many of the first colonists sent word back to England with strong advice for those who were to follow, and nearly all mentioned the necessities of adequate preparation. For example one prominent Salem minister, the Reverend Francis Higginson, wrote in 1630 that prospective colonists should "be careful to be strongly instructed what things are fittest to bring with you for your more comfortable passage at sea, as also for your husbandry occasions when you come to the land." He further warned that "for when you are once parted with England you shall meet neither markets nor fayres to buy what you want. . . ."[1] Another well-known colonist, Governor William Bradford, offered another piece of sage wisdom, this time hinting about the resolve of prospective colonists who "are too delicate and unfitte to begin new plantations and colonies that cannot endure the biting of a muskeeto."[2]

Despite what we might guess about life in seventeenth-century America, interior decoration, if it can be thought of as such, was of importance to the colonists, especially after they achieved a degree of comfort within their new surroundings. Though few English furnishings save small personal items were brought here in the crowded holds of ships during the early days, the colonists had both a need and a taste for fashionable items. More than a few were themselves skilled craftsmen and joiners well

able to construct both case and seat furniture of surprising sophistication from the vast supplies of native woods. As the century progressed and trade took hold, seaport settlements became repositories of fashionable goods and furnishings. When New Yorker Margharita van Varick died in 1696, the inventory of her estate included ebony chairs, many Chinese porcelains and lacquered trays, and several so-called "East India cabinets."[3] Thus, fashionable interiors were apparently not uncommon and prompted several writers to mention the elegance that characterized the homes of more than a few merchants. In 1700, for example, one observer wrote that "a gentleman from London would almost think himself at home in Boston . . . when he observes the number of People, their Houses, their Furniture, their tables, their Dress and Conversation, which is perhaps as splendid and showy, as that of the most considerable Tradesman in London."[4]

Throughout the eighteenth century, many Americans built and furnished houses that reflected both popular English taste and their increasing personal wealth and standard of living. In 1741, for example, Godfrey Malbone, a merchant who had grown rich from West Indian trade and privateering, built a house near Newport, Rhode Island, of pink sandstone with "the sides of the windows and the corner stones [quoins] of the house being painted like white marble."[5] Reported to have cost the then-staggering sum of £20,000, the house had interior doors of mahogany and a circular staircase that reportedly went to the attic.[6] Another wealthy colonial, Bostonian Thomas Hancock, built a magnificent mansion overlooking the Common only a few years before, in 1737. In addition to ordering window glass, marble mantelpieces, and many delft fireplace tiles from London, Hancock also instructed his agent there to send him wallpaper designed according to a sketch he had provided. He wrote that it be made "as cheap as possible, and if they can make it more beautiful by adding more Birds flying here and there, with Some Landskip at the Bottom, [I] should like it well."[7]

By the end of the eighteenth century, Americans had become well known and respected as architects, cabinetmakers, and designers and had, of course, achieved recognizable status as successful constitutional democrats and diplomats by that time, as well. Interestingly, almost all of the Founding Fathers, including Benjamin Franklin, George Washington, Thomas Jefferson, and even the dour New Englander John Adams, paid close attention to stylish household fashions. Unlike some of their other ideas, this one was not at all revolutionary, but actually the accepted practice for men of learning and sophistication. While in London in 1758, for example, Benjamin Franklin took the time to shop for a carpet "for a best room floor" and a quantity of textiles which he shipped to his wife, Deborah, in Philadelphia. So he wrote, "There is also fifty-six yards of cotton printed curiously from copperplates, a new invention, to make bed and window curtains; and seven yards chair bottoms, printed in the same way, very neat. These were my fancy; but Mrs. Stevenson [his London landlady] tells me I did wrong not to buy both of the same colour."[8] His compatriot Thomas Jefferson was also interested in textiles and not only ordered his own materials from Philadelphia, but designed the curtains into which they were to be fashioned. His instructions to a Philadelphia merchant called for "crimson damask silk lined with green and yellow fringe."[9] Times have certainly changed, and one wonders how many statesmen and politicians today have any interest in choosing the textiles for their own homes—not to mention the ability to design their own curtains.

During the nineteenth century, Americans enjoyed a great number of style options within the realm of interior decoration. In fact, the choices were so numerous that some styles lasted only a short while before being overtaken by others. By mid-century, the preponderance of classical styles, which had held sway in varying forms for nearly a century, began to yield to other styles— many of which were historic revivals. Among the most popular were the Gothic and Elizabethan Revivals, both of which existed simultaneously and were often combined in the same interior scheme. The Rococo, which was a sensuous fashion of florid S and C scrolls having little to do with the eighteenth-century style of the same name, soon gave way to a host of others, including the Renaissance Revival, a number of so-called Exotic styles, and the revivals of French forms from Louis XIII to Louis XVI. Not to be forgotten was the revival of American colonial forms—called Colonial Revival—a style that caught on with increasing strength after the Centennial celebration of 1876 and which, in some respects, has never really ended.

Despite the image most of us share of the eclectic and even haphazard mixtures of Victorian-era decorative objects, the fact is that many contemporary theorists were very strict about decoration and design. Some of the most pleasing of all late-nineteenth-century interiors were those which fall under the general rubric of the Aesthetic Movement. A reaction against the heavy decorations and general clutter characteristic of many period interiors, Aesthetic principles stressed subdued colors, simple lines, naturalistically derived decorative patterns, strains of the exotic, and a well-thought-out decorative scheme. The concept that art could be a part

of the design process was paramount. The best practitioner of these dicta in America was probably Louis Comfort Tiffany and his firm, Associated Artists. So fashionable was the Aesthetic philosophy that only six months after a general restoration of the White House, President Chester A. Arthur retained Tiffany to redesign certain rooms on the state floor. Tiffany's work is as legendary as the decorations carried out there almost seventy-five years earlier by Benjamin Henry Latrobe and Dolley Madison. Tiffany's redecoration was probably most successful in the Red Room. There, and in keeping with the room's traditional color, the walls were glazed a deep Pompeiian-red that shaded to a lighter hue as it reached the cornice. As seen in the stereoscopic photograph on page 11, the varnished-cherry fireplace was the most prominent architectural feature in the room. The firebox was lined with gleaming brass which matched the andirons and fender. A tile surround was reportedly of bright-red ceramics, and around that were squares of stained red Morocco. The large overmantel mirror was enframed with deep red plush that was in turn decorated with gilding and brightly colored glass tiles.[10] Though shown in the photograph with some items introduced by Arthur, the room was, more than anything else, intended to be a careful orchestration of color, light, and materials.

Three hundred years after the first colonists set foot upon these shores, American design and decoration had seemingly come full swing. After the excesses of the Victorian era, Americans seemed to accept a return to a simpler life—or at least the illusion of one. Perhaps most noteworthy at this time was the rise of the professional interior decorator who, unlike the upholsterers and decorators of the nineteenth century, favored a sparer elegance and a passion for exquisite, refined detailing and materials. Ogden Codman and Edith Wharton are perhaps the best known of those who championed this new outlook on houses and furnishings. Though not a decorator per se, Wharton had a lifelong interest in interior design and collaborated with Codman on *The Decoration of Houses* (1897). In her autobiography, *A Backward Glance* (1934), Wharton reminisced about her alliance with Codman and noted that they both believed "interior decoration should be simple and architectural" and that they had eschewed the common Victorianism she called "sumptuary excesses."[11]

If the interior style favored by people like Codman, Wharton, and the rest of their wealthy crowd still seemed grand, it was Gustav Stickley whose philosophies most appealed to the general population. The Craftsman style he popularized reveled in simple houses, constructed of local materials and designed for the needs of ordinary people. If these houses had anything in common with the grand houses favored by Codman and

Wharton, it was their disdain for excessive decoration. A typical Codman interior, though lavishly and correctly detailed, was sparsely furnished and decorated in comparison with its nineteenth-century couterparts. Superfluous decoration was avoided, and, as a result, the objects in the room became important objects unto themselves. The approach was much the same in the Craftsman room, with furnishings and architecture designed and detailed to fit together naturally. The practice was new, if the idea itself was not entirely so. In 1850, Andrew Jackson Downing had written that "in domestic architecture, the feeling of harmony is more demanded, and more easily evinced, in the interiors than in the exteriors of houses—because the interiors show a greater variety of lines, forms, and colors . . . Harmony is evinced in all of these cases by rejecting all forms, outlines, and colors that do not intrinsically admit of being brought into harmonious agreement with each other."[12]

Today there is more interest in the historic American interior than ever before. Much of this fervor is certainly due to the popular press, and especially to the glossy shelter magazines that illustrate historic interiors in a romantic and evocative manner appealing to us all. Still another influence is the burgeoning historic preservation movement and the growth of interest over the past three or four decades in such restored living environments as Colonial Williamsburg and Old Sturbridge Village. The careful scholarship at these places and others, the public-oriented programs they have developed, and their reproduction programs cannot be underestimated in focusing a popular spotlight on our historic patrimony.

There is, of course, a natural desire for people to want to learn about their past—especially in a climate of social change where it is felt to be slipping away so very quickly. There is a nostalgia for the past, and, though some would argue against acknowledging it too much, it would seem entirely natural and even necessary that we do so. In this regard we might do well to remember a line by Algernon Charles Swinburne in "An Ode to England" (1884): "All our past acclaims our future."[13] Indeed, most of us find our lives enriched and broadened by an understanding and appreciation of the rich heritage of our American past—architectural, decorative, and historical.

Although the first houses of the early American colonists in New England and the South were little more than rudimentary shelters, dwellings of permanence were the rule by the middle of the seventeenth century. In 1642, only twenty years after the landing at Plymouth, Edward Johnson, a newly arrived joiner, wrote that "the Lord hath been pleased to turn all the wigwams, huts and hovels the English dwelt in at their first coming, into orderly, fair and well-built houses, well furnished many of them. . . ."[1] These "fair" dwelling houses were substantially the same as those Johnson knew in rural England. Several of the earliest colonists were skillful joiners and builders and were well able to construct houses in the time-honored medieval fashion—with posts and beams and pegged connections. Of course, as in any colonial architecture, construction and design were adapted to local conditions and to the materials at hand. In New England, for example, blustery, cold, and snowy winters necessitated making the central chimney especially efficient. Adapted from the English models, these large chimneys took on an important role in New England. The New England scene pictured here depicts two types of houses seen by the middle of the seventeenth century. Most common was probably that which had one large room on the first floor with an attic or garret above. The dwelling house with two floors was surely for the more substantial family and contained one large room per floor with an attic space beneath the roof.

1
The Earliest Colonials (1650-1700)

THE TYPICAL SEVENTEENTH-CENTURY New England dwelling house was generally cramped and crowded. It was not uncommon to find extended families of ten or twelve people living together in a house that would have served best for five or six. With elderly parents, widowed parents, newly married children, and numerous offspring all living under the same roof, the privacy we take for granted today was virtually unknown. Despite such overcrowding, New Englanders took pride in their houses and, in many instances, made them into what were apparently bright and cheerful places. Although the Puritans have always been considered a dour and gloomy people, we know today that they loved bright colors. Popular colors, found both in the woolens used on bed hangings and upholstery and on the decorative champfers of posts, beams, and the shadow moldings of vertical pine paneling, were always the most fashionable.[2]

The elevation of the fireplace wall in a New England parlor, about the year 1675, above, suggests the ways in which color was used within a relatively monochromatic space. Red, or vermilion as red was often known, not only decorates the black-painted beam and paneling, but the window soffits as well. The hearth-beam molding, which imitates one originally located in Ipswich, Massachusetts,[3] is also painted black and red, but is perhaps most noteworthy because it suggests a classical stirring within a still largely medieval environment. The most formal room in a house with a separate kitchen, this type of room would have been the principal bedchamber as well as the room used for formal occasions and the entertainment of guests. Valued objects would have been part of the decoration of such a space and would have included elaborate court cupboards, leather- or embroidery-covered chairs, and expensive tables covered with turkey carpets. The adjoining kitchen, or hall, would have been a far more utilitarian chamber—the center of family life and likely the bedroom of a family member as well.

1.-3. Red, yellow, and dark-green woolens, typical of the seventeenth century, are reproduced by Textile Reproductions. 4. A betty lamp, in which a wick is placed in a reservoir of grease. The odor produced was foul, and fragrant bayberry candles were favored on special occasions. 5. Silver dram cups, similar to this seventeenth-century New England example, were small and used for consuming strong distilled alcohol. 6. Court cupboards were often made in colonial America and used for storage and the display of possessions. Bright paint often highlighted these pieces. 7. Wallpaper was rare in seventeenth-century America. Shown here is "Arlesford," an English wallpaper, c. 1690-1700. Christopher Hyland, Inc. 8. Most people ate from wooden plates and chargers called "treenware." Forks and other eating utensils were costly and rare and large linen napkins an indispensable part of every table setting. 9. Joined or "joint" stools were, after simple benches, the most common seating form in seventeenth-century colonial homes. 10. A reproduction of a mid-seventeenth-century English cradle, c. 1620, by Heart of the Wood. 11. John Milton wrote The Second Defense of the English People *in 1654, and copies would certainly have been found in several New England Puritan homes. Its theme of Christian liberty was religiously and politically based and celebrated the achievements of Cromwell and other Commonwealth leaders. 12. A standing-salt made in England mimics Dutch delftware. Salt was costly and celebrated at the table with such accessories. The knobs on top were used to hold a dish. 13. Posset pots were used for the consumption of a flavorful beverage drunk with great ceremony. This example dates from the end of the seventeenth century. 14. A Dutch delft charger decorated to imitate more costly oriental porcelains.*

Fabric background on page 15: "Somerton Damask," a design dating from c. 1630-1640 and reproduced from bed hangings made in 1680 in the antechamber to the Queen's bedchamber, Ham House, Surrey. Classic Revivals.

MANY OF AMERICA'S earliest colonists were well-educated skilled craftspeople. Not surprisingly, their sophistication was quickly evidenced in the furnishing of their homes and in the goods they brought with them and made here. The most decorative, and the most costly and valued, included brightly colored imported woolens and fine examples of woolen damasks. Used primarily for bed hangings and chair coverings, woolens were apparently not generally used as window curtains, which were rare, at least in the earliest years of settlement. Privacy was often achieved by the use of sliding interior shutters. Some accounts suggest that well-to-do families may have hung woolen hangings on their walls, either in plain solid colors or in elaborately embroidered ones, as much as for decoration as to check the incessant drafts of New England winters. The expensive damasks were very rarely seen and were probably only found in relatively small pieces used decoratively on court cupboard and chest tops.

Blessed geographically with rich arable soil and wide navigable rivers and bays, colonial Virginia became wealthy through the exportation of tobacco and the development of the plantation system. Perhaps most visually symbolic of the colony's economic and social power was the plantation manor house itself, the siting of which was invariably on a prominent hill with a vista to the wharves along the water. Surrounded as necessity required by innumerable outbuildings, the manor house became the social center of the surrounding countryside and an important landmark, particularly when seen from the water, which, not surprising in a time of poor roads, was a major social route between plantations. Brick had been a favored building material in the southern colonies from the early seventeenth century and was used both in the construction of modest dwellings and the largest public buildings. Happily, brick was well adapted to the Georgian architectural style which flourished in its own particular variant within this largest American colony. A classical style influenced by Renaissance ideals and the work of sixteenth-century Italian architects, the style was particularly appealing to the well-educated gentlemen of Virginia. An architecture of strict symmetry, it was heavily reliant upon exacting geometric proportions and relationships and was easily translated to the colonial shores through the architectural handbooks owned by many plantation owners.

2

Tidewater Manors (1700-1725)

BY THE BEGINNING of the eighteenth century, both furnishings and interiors exemplified to ever increasing degrees a turn away from medieval-inspired forms to objects of greater luxury and comfort. While rooms continued to function in multipurposed ways, the decorative arts and the architecture of the interior mirrored the fruits of the New World's material successes and their enjoyment. Not surprisingly, this new emphasis upon comfort and luxury was fittingly represented in the design of much of the seat furniture which appeared at this time. For example, caning—used on the seats and backs of chairs and daybeds—reflected the interest in comfort and portability. Like the ubiquitous daybed, the upholstered wing chair satisfied the demand for both comfort and luxury. As befitted an important southern manor house, the first-floor rooms were often embellished with fully paneled walls similar to the type shown above. Sometimes these were added after the householder's estate increased in value, since paneling was costly. Bold moldings were the most common architectural features in paneling at this time, with the prominent bolection molding most often seen at chair-rail height and around hearth openings. While these wooden features were usually painted in solid colors to imitate the color of stone or walnut, they were sometimes fashionably grained and marbleized. Paneling was almost never left in its natural state and stained, a practice that gained favor and popularity during the late nineteenth century and the subsequent Colonial-Revival period. Graining and marbleizing were often curiously juxtaposed in the same wall, regardless of the fact that the real materials would never have been combined in such a fashion. Graining to imitate cedar, as shown above, was especially popular, most likely because of cedar's rich color and exuberant graining pattern. Exemplifying the period's love of surface decoration, the high chest of drawers is richly veneered, probably with burl walnut. Prominent moldings and bulbous turned legs further characterize the period's preference for prominent detailing. A detachable set of black-painted steps surmount the chest and carries on the earlier tradition of the court cupboard for the display of decorative ceramics. The turned high-backed chair, in a style now called "William and Mary," is rendered comfortable by an upholstered back and matching cushion or "squab." A lounge by day and a sleeping couch at night, the daybed is covered in flamestitching. The walls are hung with wallpaper of a flamestitch design known to have existed at this time. Its wide heart-pine boards simply waxed, the floor is uncarpeted.

1. Books were costly and highly prized by American colonists. Like many, this book was religiously based. 2. Through their English agents, aristocratic southerners often imported large dinner services with armorial bearings from the orient. 3. Biblical and allegorical subjects were often painted on English- and Dutch-made fireplace tiles. These were not only decorative, but served a didactic role in the instruction of young children. 4. An oriental bulb pot in popular blue and white. 5. Desks such as this were produced in the colonies at this time and highly valued. 6. A baroque-style engraving from A Winter-Evening Conference Between Neighbours, 1720. Embroidery designs often incorporated similar motifs. 7. A canvas floorcloth in a fashionable wood parquet pattern. 8. Large mirrors were expensive and generally hung in locations where they could be admired and well-utilized. 9. A monteith of English origin imitating oriental porcelain and used to chill wine and punch glasses. 10. Furniture, such as this English tall case clock, was sometimes "japanned," a term applied to decorating objects with oriental motifs. Boston was a popular center for this kind of work. 11. A hand-blown wine glass. 12. Wing chairs first appeared during this period as furniture began to reflect a greater interest in comfort. This English chair is covered with green and yellow wool. 13. While silver flatware and holloware were imported, many pieces, like this sugar caster, were made in the colonies. 14. Many chairs of this style were shipped to Virginia during the first half of the eighteenth century. Generally covered in black leather and often painted red, they were made in the Boston area and are sometimes referred to as "Boston chairs."

Fabric background on page 19: A European fabric made between 1680 and 1700 and subsequently reproduced as "Gloucester Damask" by Schumacher for the Colonial Williamsburg Foundation.

By the first quarter of the eighteenth century, elegance and comfort were the hallmarks to which many prosperous Americans aspired in furnishing their homes. In the South, well-to-do planters imported many goods directly to their own docks, goods from both England and the northern colonies.

Houses with gambrel roofs, like that on the wood-framed house seen here, were considered quite stylish, especially during the first three quarters of the eighteenth century. In fact one observer noted in 1781 that it was only the gambrel-roofed houses in his New England community that were painted, a suggestion that those who owned these stylish dwelling houses were the only residents with the means to afford paint.[1] The Georgian architectural formula of rigid symmetry, classical detailing, and strict proportions was essentially identical throughout the colonies, although regional stylistic differences distinguished buildings from North and South and even from colony to colony. Double-hung sash windows were an indispensable feature of this classic American house form throughout America.

3
The Georgians (1730-1760)

WHILE THE USE OF BRIGHT color had been the hallmark of the seventeenth-century interior, by the middle of the eighteenth a well-defined "system" was practiced wherein colors were used to contrast with one another, rather than to match. In the room above, this emphasis upon contrast can be seen between the yellow woolen material used for the window festoons and upholstery, the color of the woodwork, and the wallpaper. While color contrasts often startle modern-day eyes, the practice was common during the period. The impressively paneled fireplace wall of this mid-eighteenth-century New England bedchamber reflects the classically inspired architecture of the period. Elements such as pilasters, arches with keystones, and pedimented doorways were often found in room interiors and carefully designed and proportioned according to formulas in widely circulated architectural handbooks. The dark-brown color, intended to simulate walnut and hence often known as "walnut color," is enlivened with touches of white paint to emphasize the architectural carving. The wing chair suggests the room was used as a bedchamber, the upholstered seating form being generally reserved for use in sleeping rooms. True to the custom of the day, the seat upholstery matches the fabric used on the window festoons, here shown pulled up to the window head. Not unlike a Roman shade, the festoons could be lowered to any height by affixing a cord to a knob attached at the side of the window. A bed, perhaps standing in a corner and out of view in the illustration, would have been curtained with the same yellow material, which would likely have been an imported wool. A mixture of furnishings includes an older table used as a washstand and an early eighteenth-century mirror under which a piece of linen has been tacked to protect the fashionable "Pillar and Arch"-patterned wallpaper. Since this room may have also served as a parlor for an invalid or elderly relation, a tea table and several matching side chairs in a style now called "Queen Anne" could have been placed around the perimeter of the room when not in use. As in most rooms of the period, the floor would have been uncarpeted. Possibly not even waxed, wooden floors were often merely well scrubbed and then scoured with sand or other abrasives and swept clean.

1. Handwoven woolen fringe, cord, and decorative tapes, the latter used as edging on bed hangings, upholstery, and curtains. Textile Reproductions. 2. High-style damasks such as "Godolphin Damask" were costly and even rare and, in America, generally woolen. This early-eighteenth-century fabric was originally available in both silk and wool. Classic Revivals. 3. A Newport-style open armchair covered in a wool damask, and a fashionably dressed lady in a dress made of blue-and-white flowered cotton. Both c. 1740. 4. An English veneered mirror with moveable candle arms. 5. Many highboys had scrolled tops and, sometimes, gilded finials. 6. "Walpole Damask," c. 1740, has been called one of the best documented of all eighteenth-century damasks. This fabric, of French or Italian origin, was originally made in both silk and wool and is shown in the narrow repeat that typified early work. Classic Revivals. 7. This floor canvas, imitating marble flooring, is typical in its use of bright contrasting colors and bold motifs. 8. As tea drinking became common in eighteenth-century England and America, many articles were fashioned for its use. This English salt-glazed teapot dates from c. 1730-1750. 9. New Englanders were prolific readers of sermons. This volume was originally sold by Daniel Henchman, perhaps colonial America's best-known bookseller. 10. This early-eighteenth-century walnut chair indicates a transition between the seventeenth-century joint stool and the later Queen Anne chair. 11. A typically bold-patterned and bright-colored English wallpaper, "Fiore," was made between 1750 and 1760. Christopher Hyland, Inc. 12. Fireplace tiles were highly decorative during the period. 13. Checkered material, often called "furniture check," was widely used for bed hangings, curtains, and slipcovers. Checks were both domestically made and imported. Seen here is "Country Plaid" by Scalamandré. 14. Tea tables of various forms developed to complement the social ritual of tea drinking. New England, c. 1730-1760.

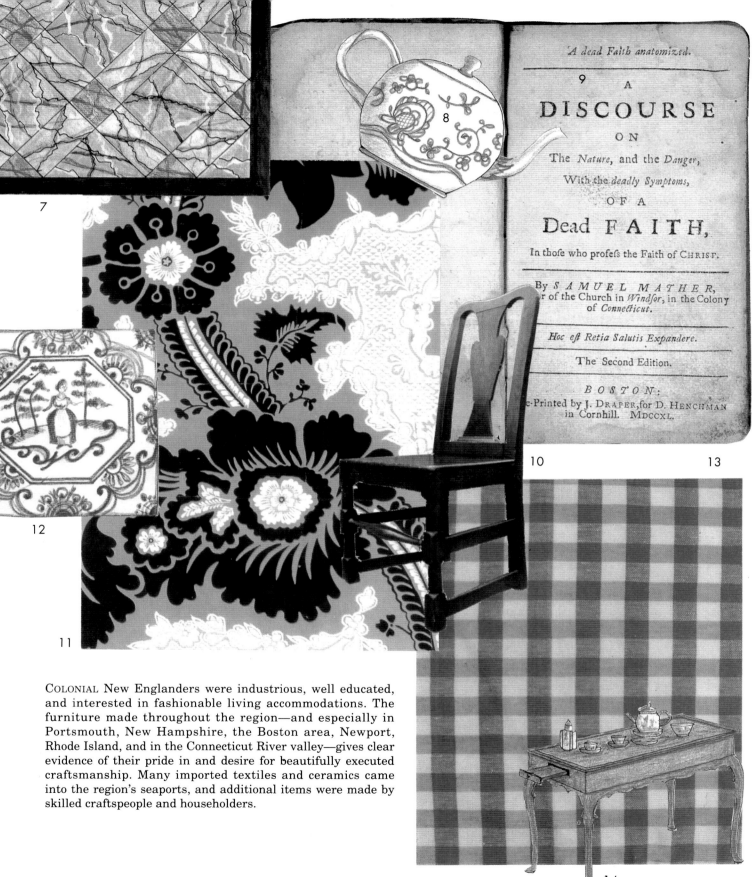

A dead Faith anatomized.

9

A

DISCOURSE

ON

The *Nature*, and the *Danger*,

With the *deadly Symptoms*,

OF A

Dead FAITH,

In thofe who profefs the Faith of CHRIST.

By *SAMUEL MATHER*,
r of the Church in *Windfor*, in the Colony
of *Connecticut*.

Hoc eft Retia Salutis Expandere.

The Second Edition.

BOSTON:
e-Printed by J. DRAPER, for D. HENCHMAN
in Cornhill. MDCCXL.

COLONIAL New Englanders were industrious, well educated, and interested in fashionable living accommodations. The furniture made throughout the region—and especially in Portsmouth, New Hampshire, the Boston area, Newport, Rhode Island, and in the Connecticut River valley—gives clear evidence of their pride in and desire for beautifully executed craftsmanship. Many imported textiles and ceramics came into the region's seaports, and additional items were made by skilled craftspeople and householders.

The social importance of the great southern plantation houses of the eighteenth century can be understood by examining those that still stand and the words that were written about them by those who lived among them. Symbolism, above all else, was an essential element in their design and setting and was well-addressed by the inate elegance and self-implied dignity of the Georgian architectural formula. This was, after all, a rational age and, perhaps more than any other house form, the plantation house was most rational of all. The fact that many of these buildings were referred to by plantation populations as "the great house" implies the prominence they had. At Nomini Hall, the Westmoreland County, Virginia, plantation of Robert Carter, the attendant structures—kitchen, workhouse, stable, and schoolhouse— were located at the corners of a large square which had at its center the great house itself. Phillip Fithian, who was tutor to the Carter children in 1773 and 1774, described the resulting triangular areas between the great house and the corner buildings as flat areas for lawn bowling, terraces, and gardens with walks of crushed oyster shells.[1] Fithian's observations about nearby Mt. Airy, the manor house of which is still standing, includes a notation about four marble statues in the garden which he called "large [and] beautiful."[2] In the view shown here, a great house, similar in scale to both Nomini Hall and Mt. Airy, stands in the middle of gardens protected from grazing animals. The approach from the main public road is along an allée of poplars, much like those described by Fithian about the Carter estate.[3]

4

Fashionable, Plain, and Neat (1760-1775)

BY THE THIRD QUARTER of the eighteenth century, America was still in many ways an outpost of the British Empire. While many British goods could be found in American homes, they were expensive and had to be ordered long in advance of their anticipated use. Wealthy planters, who often exchanged tobacco for goods, notified their factors in England when they wished to procure particular decorative objects.[4] Not surprisingly, given the distance between purchaser and seller, inferior goods were often shipped to Virginia and the other colonies to the great disappointment of plantation families and the anger of the planters themselves, George Washington included.[5] In ordering goods from abroad, planters often used the words "neat and plain" in specifying their wishes for objects in the Classical taste rather than those in the Gothic, Chinese, or Rococo modes.[6] The distance from the centers of English taste, as well as the long delay between ordering and receiving goods, made it prudent to keep things both simple and conservative. The dining room above is furnished with simple, sturdy

pieces, most of which were probably made locally, or even in the plantation carpenter's shop. The chairs were likely part of a large number used as required throughout the first-floor rooms. A gate-legged table, probably one of several like it, is here readied to accommodate five diners. For larger gatherings, the other sections would be brought in from the hallway and assembled as needed. Since sideboards were not yet in use, a marble-slabbed mixing table would have been used by serving men to place food or mix punch.[7] With floors still uncarpeted at this date, floor canvases were frequently found beneath dining room tables. The major architectural embellishments in these houses were often their paneled walls, all of which were painted, some with floral decorations.[8] Here, Ionic pilasters with gilded capitals flank a painted overmantel landscape probably painted in England expressly for the room. Most Virginian manor houses were decorated with family portraits and with sets of engravings, occasionally, as at Mount Airy, of race horses.[9]

1. *Floorcloths were fashionable and utilitarian. They were made of heavy canvas on which paint was applied. Patterns varied, with some customized for the client.* 2. *Virginian planters could afford fine furniture, and many ordered pieces from both the northern colonies and England.* 3. *"Carolina Toile" is a cotton copperplate print with Rococo decorations, c. 1775. Schumacher for the Colonial Williamsburg Foundation.* 4. *Colonial Virginians, like other colonists, loved news and gossip. This entertaining book contains an account of a thief who specialized in the theft of textiles—an indication of their value.* 5. *This English import was made for the American market, c. 1775, and took advantage of colonial political sentiment to assure its sale.* 6. *"Pillar and Arch," a scenic paper, is shown with "Egg and Dart Border" and a bright-yellow "Williamsburg Wool Moreen." "Pillar and Arch" is particularly effective in such large-scale spaces as stair halls. Schumacher.*

1

2

3

A SELECT and IMPARTIAL
ACCOUNT
OF THE
Lives, Behaviour, *and* Dying-Words,
Of the moſt REMARKABLE
CONVICTS,
From the Year 1700, down to the preſent Time.

Containing amongſt many others the following, *viz.*

Herman Strodman, for the barbarous Murder of *Peter Wolter,* his Fellow-Apprentice.
Thomas Cook, the *Gloucester* Butcher, for the Murder of Mr. *John Cooper,* a Conſtable in *May-Fair.*
John Morgridge, for the Murder of Lieut. *Cope* in the *Tower.*
Mr. *Green,* Clerk to the late ... *by Harley,* afterwards Earl of *Oxford,* for Correſponding with Her Majeſty's Enemies.
Richard Town, Tallow-Chandler, the only Per-

ſon executed on the Bankrupt Act.
Col. *Oxburgh,* Richard *Gascoigne,* Eſq; Juſtice *Hall,* and Parſon *Paul* for High-Treaſon.
Lieut. *Bird* for the Murder of *S. Loxton,* at a Bagnio.
Matthias Brinsden, for the Murder of his Wife.
James Sheppard, for imagining and compaſſing the Death of his moſt Sacred Majeſty King *George I.*
Mr. *Noble,* an Attorney, for the Murder of *John Sayer,* Eſq;

The SECOND EDITION, Corrected and Enlarged.

Fœlix quem faciunt aliena Pericula cautum.

V O L. I.

L O N D O N :

Printed by J. APPLEBEE, for CHARLES MARSH, at *Cicero's*-Head, in *Round-Court* in the *Strand.* 1745.

No Stamp Act,...

5

4

26

AMONG the most fashionable and valuable of all textiles imported to America during the eighteenth century were brightly colored woolen moreens. Moreens are distinguished by wavy, almost moiré-like, backgrounds which are additionally engraved with patterns of flowers and ribbons. Bright colors are typical, and documentary examples include crimson, yellow, blue, garnet, pink, green, purple, and even black. There is no doubt that elegant textiles like the moreen illustrated opposite would have been found in the parlors and dining rooms of the finest plantation houses. As was the fashion, the curtains would have matched the textiles used on the chairs and other seat furniture. This wool moreen is an exact reproduction of an eighteenth-century document.

Established in 1682 by William Penn, the city of Philadelphia grew by 1776 to be the second largest city in the British Empire. A conservative, peaceful city, and a center of both industry and learning, Philadelphia holds a proud place as the major center of political events leading to the Revolutionary War, and, as such, was home, if even for short periods of time, to many of America's most brilliant citizens. Like other American cities, Philadelphia by the third quarter of the eighteenth century was essentially British in appearance and, as other colonies, was imbued with its own particular brand of Georgian architecture. Dwelling houses tended to be solid, well-built, and plain—qualities which were favored by the conservative Quakers and Germans who dominated the region. In contrast, however, house interiors were often surprisingly elegant and rich. By 1776 Philadelphia was a very prosperous city, made especially so in part because of its admirable location 100 miles upriver from the ocean and yet tied to the rich resources of the Pennsylvanian heartland. Not surprisingly, Philadelphia demanded and received the best of American colonial craftsmanship.[1]

5

The Philadelphia Rococo (c. 1775)

AS THE BRITISH EMPIRE'S second largest city, Philadelphia was a major center of American furniture making and high-style decoration. The city boasted a large number of woodworkers and, during the 1760s, experienced an influx of talented and highly skilled English-born carvers and cabinetmakers. To these men is attributed the emergence and success of the rococo style in the city, a style that had enjoyed particular favor in England from the 1740s. Characterized by a preponderance of *C* and *S* scrolls, asymmetrical surface carving of exuberant naturalistic motifs, and the use of the cartouche, furniture carved in this fashion was among the most fashionable and costly.[2] Sensuous rococo decorative treatment was also found on such objects as mantelpieces and overmantels, picture frames, brass clock faces, silver and china, bookplates, and engraved and printed materials. An especially elegant, though possibly not common, American application of rococo motifs was in the decoration of flat wall surfaces. Two varieties are known to have existed in this country, although they

were more commonly found in England: rooms decorated with plain-colored papers upon which scenic designs were painted,[3] and, as shown above, rooms with both prints and decorative paper or paper-mâché scrollwork frames applied to plain painted walls or plain-colored papers. Called print rooms, chambers decorated in this second manner were often the special project of a gifted female householder who carefully assembled prints and purchased the decorative scrollwork locally.[4] Shown during the summertime, the room suggests the parlor of a Philadelphia town house. In keeping with the period's love of color contrast, the wool damask upholstery beneath the red-and-white checked slipcovers could have been in crimson, yellow, or even purple, the latter especially popular at the time when contrasted with green.[5] Matching window festoons would have been hung at each window, and a plain plastered ceiling and an uncarpeted but highly waxed floor would have presented appropriate foils to the richly carved woodwork and glowing patina of the mahogany or walnut doors.

1. This fabric, called *"Nemours Cotton and Linen Print,"* copies a documented painted linen in the Winterthur collection. The original was made in India between 1725 and 1775 and displays the popular *"Tree of Life"* motif. Brunschwig & Fils. 2. The highboy is a unique American furniture form, the best examples of which were made in Philadelphia during this period. Some, like this one, had gilded rococo finials and others even bust-finials of Voltaire and Rousseau. 3. Like this tilt-top tea table, c. 1770, Philadelphia furniture was often made of mahogany. 4. *"Floral Damask"* by Schumacher for the Colonial Williamsburg Foundation. 5. This English ceramic sauce boat displays the typical S and C scrolls that characterized rococo furniture. 6., 9. Furniture checks were commonly found in the better Philadelphia drawing rooms as a loose covering to protect costly damask upholstery. These examples are handwoven by Textile Reproductions. 7. An American-made Philadelphia side chair with a combination of rococo and Gothic elements and a red-checked seat cover. 8. As card playing became a popular pastime, many eighteenth-century Americans considered the sport a particular vice. This card table has a green baize playing surface. 10. A late-eighteenth-century Chinese-export teacup. 11. An English-made ceramic teapot in the so-called *"Chintz"* pattern. 12. Voltaire was especially revered by well-educated Americans. This volume was originally owned by a gentleman in nearby Wilmington, Delaware.

THE
WORKS
OF
M. DE VOLTAIRE.

TRANSLATED FROM THE FRENCH.

WITH

NOTES, HISTORICAL AND CRITICAL.

BY T. SMOLLETT, M.D.

T. FRANCKLIN, M.A. AND OTHERS.

IN TWENTY-FOUR VOLUMES.

VOLUME V.

THE FOURTH EDITION.

DUBLIN:
PRINTED BY R. MARCHBANK,
FOR R. MONCRIEFFE IN CAPEL-STREET.
M,DCC,LXXII.

PHILADELPHIA was one of the British Empire's most important cities. Because of its excellent harbor and rich surrounding countryside, it became a center of fashionable eighteenth-century life. The Rococo style, which was especially popular in England, gained a firm foothold in Philadelphia, where many of America's finest examples of the style were created.

Farmhouses have taken many forms throughout the course of American architectural history and, depending upon the prosperity of the farmer, were of varying styles and sizes by the end of the eighteenth century. Some of course were as large and imposing as Mount Vernon, while others were small and simple log cabins on the edges of settlement. The Federal-style house depicted below suggests the home of a prosperous agricultural family at the end of the eighteenth century. In New England, houses were often attached to barns and stables as a means of alleviating the need to trek outdoors during harsh and stormy weather.[1]

6
Farmers' Formal (1800-1840)

FEW DECORATIVE DEVICES found on the walls of eighteenth and early-nineteenth-century houses are as charming or evocative of the tastes of early occupants than wall paintings. Widely popular until about 1840, these decorations include several major types.[2] The first, illustrated above, consisted of freehand painting intended to imitate popular stamped or printed wallpapers. Generally seen with repeating patterns, as were wallpapers, such painted designs usually display border motifs inspired by the narrow wallpaper borders popular at the time. Freehand wall painting was usually part of the wider repertoire of the house painter during the late eighteenth and early nineteenth centuries. Naturally, styles and the quality of workmanship varied from painter to painter, with certain artisans in great demand, judging from the fact that their extant work is heavily concentrated in various regional locales.[3] Generally less rigid or static than stenciled walls which appeared concurrently, freehand wall painting was most often lucid and flowing. Often executed in floral motifs, each spray and bloom differs slightly from the next one and is usually characterized by robust brush strokes, as opposed to the dainty, carefully applied decorations of traditional hand-painted Chinese wallpapers. Freehand wall paintings were probably not directly copied from wallpaper designs but rather from fabrics which have themselves been the traditional inspiration for the design of wallpaper itself.[4]

The room illustrated here, and shown in the summertime, represents the major wall of a New England farmhouse parlor at the beginning of the nineteenth century. The buff-colored walls were a popular choice among freehand painters, although other popular colors included white, gray, yellow, bright blue, and even bright raspberry pink.[5] A large bouquet of greens—probably aromatic herbs—fills the fireplace opening, a common treatment when fireboards were not used. Simple green-painted Windsor chairs and a maple or cherry tilt-top tea table stand around the room's perimeter—the typical placement of furniture in a room not being used for a specific purpose.

1. Handwoven woolens by Textile Reproductions. 2. This pronouncing dictionary, printed in New York in 1815, reflects a growing recognition of a particularly American English. 3. A selection of books printed in America during the first decades of the nineteenth century. 4. A. J. Downing illustrated a chair made from a barrel in The Architecture of Country Houses (1850), but the idea was not new. 5. Americans celebrated Thanksgiving Day long before it became an official annual holiday in 1863. The illustration is from Charles Goodrich's The Universal Traveler (1838). Note the window curtains, chairs, and tablecloth shown in the view. 6. The Moral Instructor was intended for use in schools and homes. This copy, published in 1835, was particularly well used. 7. Colorful Venetian carpets were common in rural American homes. Loomed in strips, sewn together, and often tacked down over padding wall to wall, they were usually replaced with straw matting in summertime. The example shown is woven by Thistle Hill Weavers. 8. Windsor chairs were popular well into the nineteenth century. Most were painted. 9. This New England cherry candlestand, c. 1810, has a handsome carved shaft of acanthus and pineapple motifs. Its top tilts so that it can be placed out of the way against a wall when not in use. 10. This French cotton is called "Andrew Jackson Chintz" and dates from between 1795 and 1810. Scalamandré.

THE HOUSES of prosperous farm families were typically furnished with a variety of objects, including simple utilitarian furniture, inherited family pieces, new furniture of local origin, and domestic and imported fabrics. Housewives often wove their own carpets. Books were highly prized, and family members passed many evenings at their leisure while one of their own read aloud.

While the typical domestic house form—that of two stories, five bays, and a central doorway—persisted in America well into the nineteenth century, subtle stylistic changes began to be seen during the last two decades of the 1700s. Neoclassic detailing, largely encouraged as a result of archaeological and architectural discoveries in both Italy and Greece, came to be appreciated and understood in ways unknown to the Renaissance and Palladian architects whose work had been popular in eighteenth-century America. Fine detailing, well-proportioned elements of elegant richness which were often played against subdued backgrounds, and a general attenuation of architectural features became the hallmarks of this new style. Characterized by an overall feeling of lightness and grace, the style is best known as "Federal" because of its development during the early years of the new United States.[1] The country house shown here represents an example of the Federal style, especially popular in Boston but also common in other states. One of the most striking differences from buildings of the older Georgian style is the use of both oval and octagonal room shapes in conjunction with elegant elliptical staircases which rise from the first to the second floor, often treated as piano-nobili *and containing the main entertaining rooms.*

7

Designs for a Young Republic (1790-1820)

WHILE NEOCLASSICAL or Federal-style interior room arrangements tended to remain symmetrical, room forms often exhibited a variety of geometric shapes not seen before in America. Of course this sophistication was most commonly—if not exclusively—found in the most prominent buildings and dwelling houses wherein spaces with oval, rounded, or octagonal shapes were deemed appealing by a style-conscious class.[2]

Designed to shine with elegance, the octagonal chamber above might have been called a "ballroom," "supper room," or "drawing room" by its inhabitants and was clearly intended as a special place, made particularly so because of its form and decoration. Apart from its rather spare and simple architectural detailing, the most elaborate feature of which is the fanlighted double door, the room's most decorative elements are its wallpaper, wallpaper borders, and draperies. Similar to the popular,

though costly, French wallpapers by Jean-Baptiste Réveillon and others, the wallpaper illustrated displays the Pompeiian colors and motifs that had been discovered on the walls and mosaics of contemporary archaeological sites.[3] A suite of green-painted "fancy furniture," which includes chairs and window seats, suggests that the room may have been intended for dancing and receptions where easily movable furniture was preferred. Two fine pier tables, inspired by one made in New York around 1805, and two matching looking glasses from the same locale and period, flank the doorway. In the center of the room, a lolling, or so-called "Martha Washington," armchair, slipcovered with a green-and-white striped cotton, is drawn up to a worktable. A small haircloth-covered footstool sits nearby upon a bare wooden floor that has been decoratively banded with a green stripe.[4]

1. The colors of the wallpaper "Bernardston" suggest the vibrant palette of a young America. The motifs and banding are typical of the Federal era. Schumacher. **2.** Even bookplates evoked classical designs. **3.** The door from the interior of an American slant-top desk, c. 1800. The elongated oval, inlaid banding, and stained wood decoration are common period motifs. **4.** "Classical Urn" is a reproduction of one of the popular French wallpapers that found favor in an America taken with neoclassicism. Schumacher. **5.** "Pompeiian Figures" is a brightly colored carpet with colors typical of the period. J. R. Burrows and Company. **6.** "America Representing at the Altar of Liberty Medallions of Her Illustrious Sons" is a highly patriotic fabric rich in classical references. Here Washington is crowned with laurel. Scalamandré. **7, 8, 10.** American furniture of the period showcased the decorative use of shields, urns, swags, and eagles. **9.** A carpet of delicate, flowing pattern called "Pembroke Leaf," c. 1800, epitomizes Federal grace. J. R. Burrows and Company.

IT IS DESIRED THAT THIS BOOK SHOULD
BE READ ATTENTIVELY,
USED WITH CARE,
AND RETURNED
SEASONABLY
TO
HUGH RUNYAN.

THE ARCHITECTURE, furniture, and decorative arts of the Federal period in America exemplified the strong national interest in classical design motifs. Archaeological excavations fueled a resurgence of interest in classical forms and were especially appropriate symbols during the genesis of the young republic. All of the items on these pages, including even the mundane book plate (figure 2), display their debt to this new classical influence.

Many prominent and influential Americans, including Thomas Jefferson and James and Dolley Madison, were among those who recognized the very substantial talents of architect Benjamin Henry Latrobe.[1] Born and educated in England, Latrobe arrived in the new republic in 1796 at the age of 32 and was quickly appreciated both for his keen understanding of classical and current European styles and for his background in civil engineering. Among the extant buildings he designed are the Philadelphia Waterworks (1800-02), the Roman Catholic Cathedral of Baltimore (1805-21), and a Washington, D.C., town house built for Stephen Decatur (1818-19). Latrobe was familiar with the elements of neoclassical structures and understood the archaeological aspects of Greek architecture, both of which transformed the preeminent Federal style into one of special force and dignity. His work was perhaps most engaging in his domestic designs, among which was a Philadelphia town house for William and Mary Waln completed in 1808. Depicted in the drawing above, which is itself based on a watercolor view of the house done in 1847, the Waln house is evocative of French neoclassical design, especially in the presence of two flanking pavilions at each front corner.[2] Though the house is no longer standing, the elegant Greek-inspired furniture that Latrobe designed for its drawing room still exists and allows us to envision interiors that were like nothing ever seen in America before.[3]

8

The Nation's Architect (c. 1810)

THE HOUSE Benjamin Henry Latrobe designed for the Walns (facing page) was not only stylish from the exterior, but had a carefully designed and beautifully executed interior. In fact, it is likely that Latrobe's work for the Walns, and especially his designs for their drawing room in 1808, made him the logical choice as interior designer for the Oval Salon (now the Blue Room) of the White House the following year. As he had for the Walns, Latrobe provided James and Dolley Madison with a drawing room decorated in the fashionable and nationally appropriate Greek style, wherein furnishings, decorative objects, and colors were all carefully orchestrated to create a room of dazzling splendor and republican symbolism.[4] This was perhaps best illustrated in the furniture, all of which was designed by the architect. The suite consisted of thirty-six cane-seated side chairs, two long sofas, and four window seats. The chairs and sofas were painted and grained in imitation of mahogany and decorated with representations of laurel leaves and American shields. The window seats were painted white and embellished with gilded decorations.[5] In addition to placement in the window openings flanking the central window used as a door on the south wall, these were also designed to fill similar openings on the north wall. Since Latrobe ordered five pairs of window curtains for the room, historians believe these "niches," as they appear on an early plan, were actually designed to look like the windows on the south wall, with mirrors in divided sash. Between them was a double doorway leading to the hall.[6] Though Latrobe believed the bright crimson velvet curtains (he had wanted red silk damask) would ruin his reputation, they were what many observers marveled at the most.[7] The material was also used as cushions for the chairs and sofas, while the window seats were covered in blue silk. Little is known about the carpet used in the room except that Latrobe ordered 169 yards of Brussels carpet, 30 yards of carpet border, and one large matching hearth rug.[8] Whatever its design, it must have coordinated handsomely with the room's decorative scheme. Unfortunately, all of this splendor was short-lived and totally destroyed when, in August, 1814, Washington was invaded by the British and the White House burned down to its exterior walls.[9]

1. Latrobe designed this sofa with decidedly Roman features for the Oval Salon in 1809. It is almost identical in dimensions to a surviving sofa designed for the Walns the year before that is over eight and a half feet long. The original drawings for Latrobe's White House furniture are at the Maryland Historical Society. 2. The Latrobe chimneypiece complemented the Oval Salon's furnishings and colors precisely. The large mirror that had been ordered for the overmantel broke in transit and two smaller ones had to be substituted. The cornice at the top was probably made of cloth, weighted with gilded balls, and likely matched the window cornices. Original drawing by Latrobe in the Library of Congress. 3. John Burrows of J. R. Burrows and Company furnished this original pinpoint drawing of a carpet design by I. Arbuthnot, c. 1805, now in the archives of Woodward Grosvenor and Company, Ltd. Some speculate that Latrobe may have used a carpet designed by Arbuthnot for the Oval Salon, and this design would certainly have met all his requirements.[11] 4. There were "36 cane seat chairs made to a Grecian model, painted, gilded, and varnished, with the United States arms painted on each," provided for the room. The arms would have been painted on the rear of the chair's top rail and the chairs lined up around the walls of the room. John and Hugh Finlay of Baltimore are believed to have decorated the furniture. The chairs had cushions of the same red velvet used for the curtains. The original drawing for the chair is in the collection of the Maryland Historical Society.

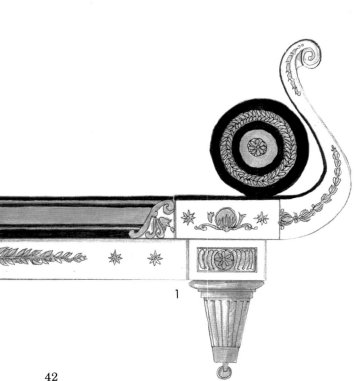

1

2

3

4

LIKE OTHER architects of his era, Benjamin Henry Latrobe was also a competent interior designer—-and even a furniture designer— and created elegant room.settings for some of America's most illustrious citizens. Unfortunately, nothing that Latrobe created for the Madison White House in 1809 survived the fire that destroyed the mansion in 1814. However, his drawings for the furniture, correspondence with its makers and the Madisons, as well as several period accounts by visitors—most of whom had never seen anything quite like it—do survive and give us a relatively clear image of how the Oval Salon must have appeared.

America has always enjoyed a special relationship with the sea. For the first two centuries of American settlement, major social and economic centers were located along the eastern seaboard, or within a short distance from the coastline. By the end of the eighteenth century and the early years of the nineteenth, many seaside towns were dominated by the large and imposing homes of shipowners and merchants whose wealth came from whaling or from trade with Europe and the Orient. The evocative widows' walks that crowned their roofs are symbolic of this link to the sea and of the owners' need to keep a watchful eye on their commercial interests. Other citizens, very much in the majority, were engaged as shopkeepers, craftsmen, and clerks and built smaller homes, many of which were places of business as well as residences. While less imposing than those of their more prosperous townsmen, these small houses or cottages were often charming and picturesque. The small house shown below suggests the residence and attached shop of a craftsman and is built just at the slope of a hill overlooking the town and port.

9

Pineapples, Starbursts, and Swags (1810-1840)

STENCILING THE WALLS OF ROOMS has a long American tradition. While the period of its greatest popularity was roughly between 1810 and 1840, the craft is thought to have been practiced at least during the last few years of the eighteenth century.[1] Stencil cutouts, usually cut into heavy cardboard or paper by the stenciler, were kept flat and stiff by the repeated application of shellac and paint. When old stencils wore out, they were simply traced onto new cardboard before being discarded.[2] Although the designs used by stencil artists varied from painter to painter, most favored designs included fans—usually used at the corners of borders—floral sprays, pineapples, and sunbursts, the last usually looking like large daisies. Urns, swags, and willows were also popular and echoed the decorative preferences of the Federal style. The stenciled room illustrated above is unusual because the background color is blue, a color not particularly popular with stencilers.[3] Far more commonly seen are a variety of yellows—from buffs and ochres to surprisingly bright butter yellow—various shades of rose, medium-toned grays, and even shades of peach. One artist is known to have stenciled directly onto unpainted wood,[4] and several stenciled walls have been found where the background color was either painted white or was merely unpainted plaster. Laying out a wall to be stenciled was an important task since the artist had to take into account the interruption of doors, windows, fireplaces, corner cupboards, and other architectural features. Conceivably, the choice of stencils used and their size were dependent upon the sizes of the wall surfaces available and their relation to one another and to the room's architectural elements. The brightly colored parlor above features a mixture of country furniture. A Chippendale-style Connecticut-made side chair, possibly one of a pair, is pulled up to a maple or cherry tea table covered with a white linen cloth or napkin to protect the surface from the redware tea articles. A green-painted Windsor armchair has a red wool cushion which matches the slipcovered seat on the side chair. Since it is summer, the fireplace has been covered over with a louvered fireboard. A well-worn child's chair, already antique by this time, stands between the fireplace and a brightly painted and grained corner cupboard filled with an accumulation of ceramic wares. Although the woodwork is predominantly of mid-eighteenth-century design, the room has been modernized with the addition of a new door, accents of graining, and an up-to-date stenciled design of pineapples and stars beneath a bright red swag motif mimicked by a similar swag hung at the window. A typical black-painted baseboard is also seen here. Typically the ceiling would have been painted white and the floor left bare, except, perhaps, in winter.

1. Chinese ceramics, like this plate in the popular "Blue Canton Willow" pattern, were shipped to America in large quantities and in several grades from the end of the eighteenth century. 2. Seafaring men brought back many wonderful and unfamiliar souvenirs. "Bali" is a reproduction of a hand-printed batik from nineteenth-century Java. Schumacher. 3. A map of the Western or Atlantic Ocean "with an illustration of the character and rout of a storm which occurred on the American coast in August, 1830," published by G. W. Blunt, 1831. 4. An illustration referring to plane sailing from The New American Practical Navigator by Nathaniel Bowditch, New York, 1826. 5. An engraving of Captain James Riley from his book, An Authentic Narrative of the Loss of the American Brig Commerce . . . , New York, 1818. 6. "La Danse Egyptienne," a toile first printed in Alsace in 1827. The scene depicts the residence of Quasim Bey in Cairo and represents the interest in exotic lands popular at the period. Classic Revivals. 7. "Pillar," a reproduction of an English fabric, c. 1815-1830. Scalamandré. 8. A New England maple tilt-top tea table, c. 1780-1800. 9. Many seafarers' trunks yield interiors lined with wallpaper. 10. The Universal Traveller by Charles A. Goodrich was published in 1838 and popular with those unable to travel to far-off lands. 11. An engraving from the latter. 12. A "tabernacle" or pier mirror probably made in eastern New York State or western Massachusetts about 1820.

The background paper on page 47 is a typical marbled paper of the period. Papers simulating marble were sometimes used below chair rails in hallways and staircases.

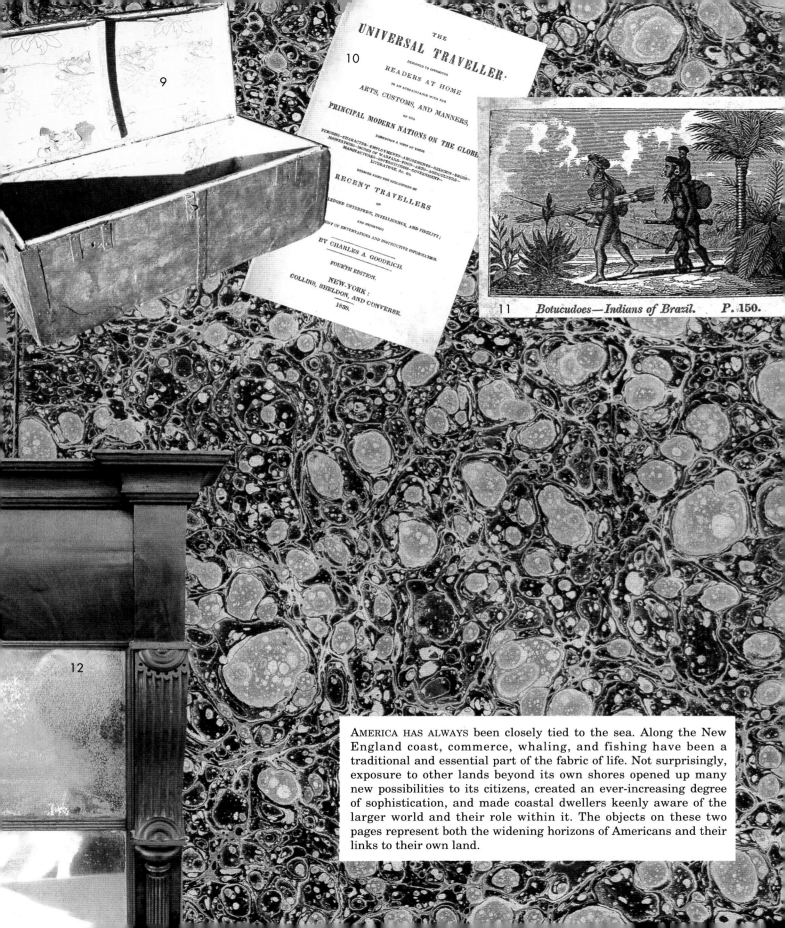

THE
UNIVERSAL TRAVELLER.
DESIGNED TO INTRODUCE
READERS AT HOME
TO AN ACQUAINTANCE WITH THE
ARTS, CUSTOMS, AND MANNERS,
OF THE
PRINCIPAL MODERN NATIONS ON THE GLOBE.
EMBRACING A VIEW OF THEIR
PERSONS—CHARACTER—EMPLOYMENTS—AMUSEMENTS—RELIGION—DRESS—
HABITATIONS—MODES OF WARFARE—FOOD—ARTS—AGRICULTURE—
MANUFACTURES—SUPERSTITIONS—GOVERNMENT—
LITERATURE, &c. &c.

DERIVED FROM THE RESEARCHES OF
RECENT TRAVELLERS
OF
ACKNOWLEDGED ENTERPRISE, INTELLIGENCE, AND FIDELITY;
AND EMBODYING
AN ACCOUNT OF ENTERTAINING AND INSTRUCTIVE INFORMATION.

BY CHARLES A. GOODRICH.

FOURTH EDITION.

NEW-YORK:
COLLINS, SHELDON, AND CONVERSE.
1838.

Botucudoes—Indians of Brazil.   P. 150.

AMERICA HAS ALWAYS been closely tied to the sea. Along the New England coast, commerce, whaling, and fishing have been a traditional and essential part of the fabric of life. Not surprisingly, exposure to other lands beyond its own shores opened up many new possibilities to its citizens, created an ever-increasing degree of sophistication, and made coastal dwellers keenly aware of the larger world and their role within it. The objects on these two pages represent both the widening horizons of Americans and their links to their own land.

Inns, public houses, and taverns were important cultural and social centers through-out the American colonies and in the young republic. Varying in size and quality, they were of necessity most always located at town centers and along main-traveled roads. As such, they functioned as meeting places for local organizations and gathering spots for political discussions. Some were small, though many, it seems, were big enough to provide a large room suitable for gatherings of some size. Public houses and inns were always domestic in appearance. Many, in fact, were private dwelling houses before they became inns. Most successful, however, were usually recognizable for what they were since they were invariably large and imposing structures. Many had three floors beneath their roofs and porches along their fronts where people waited for stages which made these places regular stops.

10

Outdoors/Indoors (1800-1840)

IN ADDITION TO freehand designs and stenciled decorations, a third variety of painted wall decoration was common, at least in New England, during the first decades of the nineteenth century. Termed variously "scenic wall murals," "scenic panoramas," and "landscape wall paintings," these designs differ from those discussed earlier by being lively representations of flora and fauna, both real and imagined. While many of the scenes which were painted onto the walls of parlors, dining rooms, and assembly rooms were realistic enough and often represented the neighboring landscape, many were colorful vistas of fantastic tropical settings full of fiery volcanoes and verdant palm trees—things local patrons could only imagine.[1] While painting scenery onto American walls is known to have occurred at least as early as the middle of the eighteenth century, the greatest influence upon the work of scenic mural painters was certainly fashionable scenic wallpapers. Largely imported and expensive, these papers were made mostly in France by such makers as Dufour and Zuber and featured the type of exotic scenery which appealed to wealthy and educated Americans.[2] One such paper, "Vues de l'Amerique du Nord," made by the firm of Zuber in Alsace, is probably the best known to Americans since an original set has now been installed in the White House.[3] The panoramic scene displayed in the room above is a representation of the type of painted landscape murals popular during the first decades of the

nineteenth century. Depicting what is intended to be a local scene, the hypothetical artist has also included a painting of a large vase of everblooming flowers and vines over the mantle shelf. A stenciled border of scrolls, vines, and flower buds is shown at the cornice line, as evidence that scenic painters often used stencils for certain aspects of their compositions.[4] The room itself represents a large public room in an inn early in the nineteenth century and is almost a total product of the abilities of the decorative painter. The painted fancy furniture, consisting of a matched set of side chairs and a settee (probably one of two), are shown pushed against the walls, sheathed to chair-rail height with horizontal boards painted a light gray or stone color. A painted worktable, with either stenciled or hand-painted decorations, is shown before a window alongside a bright-red chair probably belonging to another set elsewhere in the building. The simple red wool swag over the window is only decorative, the exterior window shutters used, as usual, to regulate heat and light. The black-painted baseboard is known to have had a long tradition of use in America as a practical deterrent against unsightly scuff-marks. As in most rooms of the period, the floors would still have been bare and possibly even unwaxed. Simple rag or list carpets, loomed in strips and then sewn together, were often used in wintertime and were sometimes even tacked down to the floor and laid wall to wall.[5]

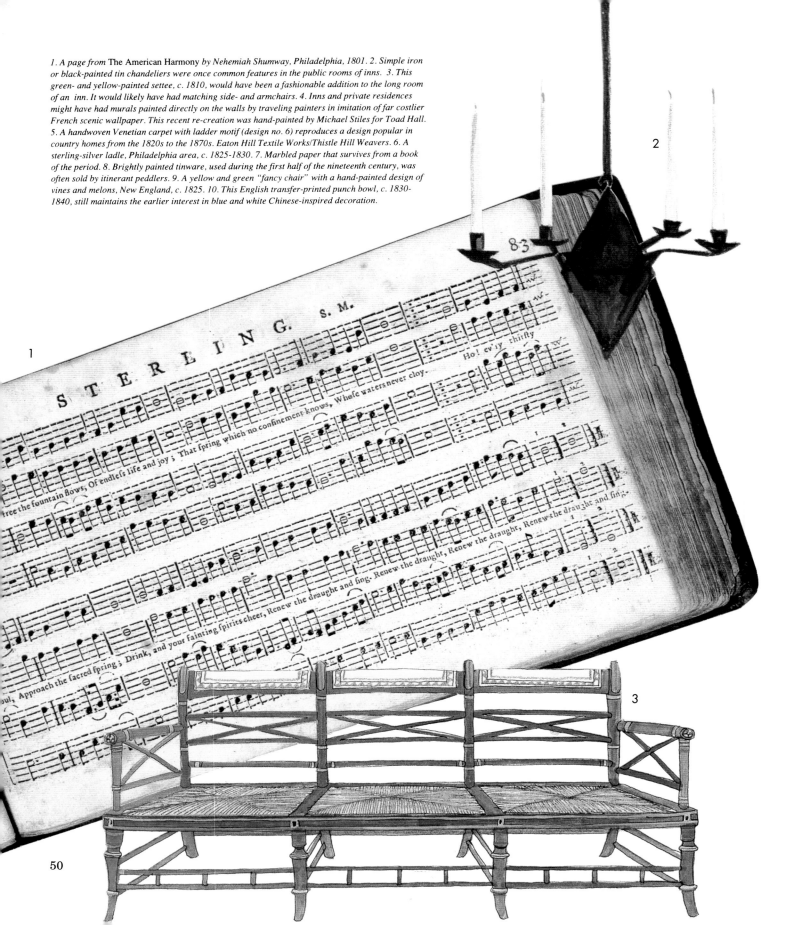

1. A page from The American Harmony by Nehemiah Shumway, Philadelphia, 1801. 2. Simple iron or black-painted tin chandeliers were once common features in the public rooms of inns. 3. This green- and yellow-painted settee, c. 1810, would have been a fashionable addition to the long room of an inn. It would likely have had matching side- and armchairs. 4. Inns and private residences might have had murals painted directly on the walls by traveling painters in imitation of far costlier French scenic wallpaper. This recent re-creation was hand-painted by Michael Stiles for Toad Hall. 5. A handwoven Venetian carpet with ladder motif (design no. 6) reproduces a design popular in country homes from the 1820s to the 1870s. Eaton Hill Textile Works/Thistle Hill Weavers. 6. A sterling-silver ladle, Philadelphia area, c. 1825-1830. 7. Marbled paper that survives from a book of the period. 8. Brightly painted tinware, used during the first half of the nineteenth century, was often sold by itinerant peddlers. 9. A yellow and green "fancy chair" with a hand-painted design of vines and melons, New England, c. 1825. 10. This English transfer-printed punch bowl, c. 1830-1840, still maintains the earlier interest in blue and white Chinese-inspired decoration.

Country inns and taverns of the eighteenth and nineteenth centuries were places of rest and relaxation and centers for lively meetings and entertainments. Since they were invariably located at the village crossroads and along busy highways, the most prominent were centers of information where local and national news could be shared. Of course the quality and the services provided by these hostelries varied from one to the other, just as is true of hotels and inns today. The best offered clean private rooms for ladies, good food, elegant furnishings, and well-appointed public rooms. The objects on these pages are among the kinds of decorative pieces that would have been commonly found in many of the finest early-nineteenth-century taverns.

Outdoors/Indoors 51

In the typical New England house, the kitchen, buttery, and woodshed were often located in an extension or ell built at the rear and perpendicular to the main body of the dwelling. This was a convenient arrangement, for it gave the farm wife a good view of distant fields in two opposite directions and provided good cross ventilation during the summer months. As shown below, a small kitchen garden for essential herbs and root vegetables was conveniently situated just outside the kitchen door as an auxiliary to a larger vegetable garden planted elsewhere. Throughout the year, as time permitted, countless cords of wood would also have been seen by the kitchen door, stacked in readiness for splitting and transferral to the woodshed. The New England ell and its relationship to outdoor spaces enables us to better understand an earlier generation's need for long-term preparation, both for warmth and the need for sufficient provisions to keep families fed throughout long winters.

11

Home and Hearth (1800-1840)

THE ROOM PICTURED ABOVE suggests the appearance of a New England kitchen about the year 1825. Furnished primarily as a workroom, it nonetheless imparts some of the attributes of a sitting room where, especially during winter evenings, family members gathered around the fire to read, talk, plan, mend, and knit. The most common article of kitchen furniture was the table—one with a well-scrubbed top that served double duty for both the preparation of meals and for dining. Chairs (some now stools because of broken backs and probably mostly mismatched), benches, a rocking chair (especially popular by about 1825), and a high-backed wooden bench known as a settle were additional furnishings. Contemporary accounts have noted that desks and bookcases also appeared in kitchens,[1] the first to provide a convenient area to conduct business and the other as a storage area for the books and newspapers providing the family with much of its evening recreation. Other accounts note that clocks were also prevalent.[2] In addition, of course, were the hosts of utilitarian objects ranging from the woodbox to cooking utensils. Kitchen walls seem to have most often been whitewashed, although evidence exists that some were painted. Since the kitchen was in most homes the most frequently used room in the house, this should not be surprising. Walls were also occasionally painted yellow. In 1845, for example, one Elizabeth Ellicot Lea provided a recipe for a yellow-ochre wash "suitable for kitchen [walls]."[3] One pleasant color that apparently enjoyed a surprising popularity, judging from old kitchens where shades of the color have been found, was a light pink or salmon, a hue represented by the warm, mottled, and faded color on the walls of the kitchen shown above. Especially popular, it seems, during the late-eighteenth and early-nineteenth centuries, walls of this color have been recently restored to the kitchen of the Gardner-Pingree House (c. 1804-1806) in Salem, Massachusetts. Color, incidentally, was also sometimes applied to kitchen floors, though most were merely well-scrubbed and sanded.

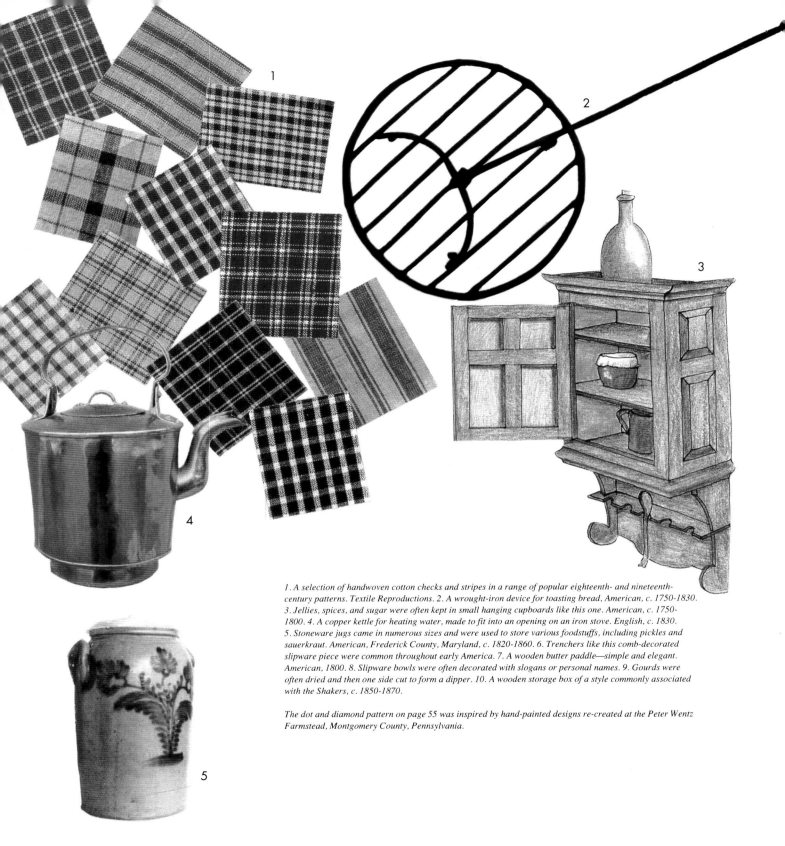

1. A selection of handwoven cotton checks and stripes in a range of popular eighteenth- and nineteenth-century patterns. Textile Reproductions. 2. A wrought-iron device for toasting bread, American, c. 1750-1830. 3. Jellies, spices, and sugar were often kept in small hanging cupboards like this one. American, c. 1750-1800. 4. A copper kettle for heating water, made to fit into an opening on an iron stove. English, c. 1830. 5. Stoneware jugs came in numerous sizes and were used to store various foodstuffs, including pickles and sauerkraut. American, Frederick County, Maryland, c. 1820-1860. 6. Trenchers like this comb-decorated slipware piece were common throughout early America. 7. A wooden butter paddle—simple and elegant. American, 1800. 8. Slipware bowls were often decorated with slogans or personal names. 9. Gourds were often dried and then one side cut to form a dipper. 10. A wooden storage box of a style commonly associated with the Shakers, c. 1850-1870.

The dot and diamond pattern on page 55 was inspired by hand-painted designs re-created at the Peter Wentz Farmstead, Montgomery County, Pennsylvania.

As the United States became more politically and economically established during the first decades of the nineteenth century, Americans sought out symbols which embodied their national ideals. The architecture of classical Greece was therefore a logical choice. Not only was this architecture tied to the birthplace of democracy, but it also offered a bold, majestic, and dignified appearance—the most appropriate style for a rapidly developing country increasingly concerned with its democratic image. Particularly popular during the 1830s and '40s, the Greek Revival style was ideally suited for public buildings, although application of Greek Revival elements on domestic buildings provided the style with its most widespread use. While the great columned mansions and pedimented temple-style houses of the South are most usually associated with it, the Greek Revival style was at its most charming when used on smaller, modestly scaled houses. In urban settings like New York City, where it was especially in vogue, Greek Revival architecture took the form of brick-faced row houses without monumental freestanding columns.[1] These row houses, many of which are extant, were usually four floors over a ground-floor basement. Greek-style architectural detailing was most often applied as porch columns, door and window surrounds, simple and bold wooden cornices, and on the detailing of cast-iron rails and fences which typically featured anthemia, running key motifs, and other designs derived from the ancients.

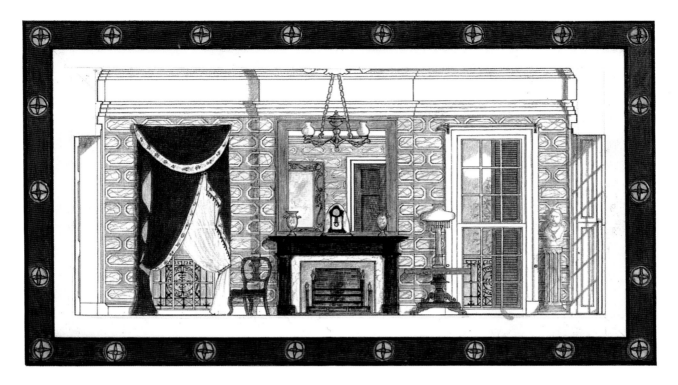

12

The Greek Revival (1830-1845)

THE INTERIOR ILLUSTRATED above represents the back or rear parlor of a corner-lot Greek-Revival town house. Most New York town houses at this time were constructed with two rooms and a narrow hallway on each floor. The dining room usually occupied the street-front room in the half basement (there was often a subbasement below this) with the kitchen to the rear. On the first or parlor floor were the front and back parlors, the latter sometimes used for dining on formal occasions. Second- and third-floor rooms contained family bedrooms, and the fourth or attic floor, a number of small rooms for servants and a drying room for laundry. As the most important public rooms in the house, the double parlors were invariably the most highly ornamented. Of equal size, they were usually separated by a wall in which were a highly polished pair of wooden sliding doors, sometimes flanked by freestanding columns which, in turn, were flanked by pilasters at the room's corners. Elaborate plaster cornices and moldings crowned the rooms which were often twelve or even fourteen feet in height. On these parlor floors, window sills were often dropped to the floor level, giving further proportional punctuation to these already grand spaces. Mantelpieces were often bold and chaste and sometimes made of beautifully figured black marble veined with

gold. Although the room above is shown being readied for summertime, the majority of the unseen furniture would have been bought in suites of matching pieces.[1] In most rooms, center tables were necessary forms, especially in rooms which served as family parlors. As a protection for their tops, they were often covered with cloths or, as shown, with green wool baize. Portraits of family members and oil paintings of landscape views would have been appropriate and typical additions in both parlors. While walls were often painted in tones of white, very light grays, or even light straw to complement the white-painted woodwork, the use of wallpaper was not uncommon at this time.[2] In the parlor shown, the walls have been hung with wallpaper in a block-like design, the center of each block containing a marbleized panel. Usually considered an appropriate paper for use in hallways, the paper was also valued in parlors.[3] Of course both parlors would have been papered identically. The cornices are here shown painted to match the woodwork, although they could have been colored in subtle, graded shades of gray. The entablature, the area between the cornices, is shown covered with a border paper. Period paintings show similar rooms carpeted with patterns that to modern eyes seem in competition with the room's wallpaper.

1. Appleton's monument and its surrounding Greek-style fence at Boston's Mount Auburn Cemetery. 2. Andrew Jackson was the popular hero of the War of 1812 and president from 1829 to 1837. 3. This fine reproduction of horsehair upholstery material is from Old World Weavers. 4. "Palmerston Damask," a wood and silk textile, is a reproduction of a fabric used in a c. 1840 curtain. Classic Revivals. 5. Inexpensive pine chairs like this one in the Classical/Empire style were made in New England and often grained to imitate rosewood. 6. Tassels, fringe, and other passementerie were indispensable drapery accompaniments. 7. An American frieze paper, c. 1840-1870. Mt. Diablo Handprints. 8. "Neoclassic Scroll," a carpet border designed in 1839. J. R. Burrows and Company. 9. This detail from a c. 1835 pier mirror shows Classical/Empire motifs including an inlaid lyre and acanthus stalks.

GREEK-REVIVAL INTERIORS like exteriors, are easily identifiable by pilasters, columns, bold and often flat-profiled cornices, and generally chaste classical elements. The most elegant interiors are characterized by exceedingly rich and handsome detailing, often carefully copied from such pattern books as Minard Lafeber's *The Young Builder's General Instructor* (1829) which disseminated the general design elements far beyond the fashionable eastern cities where the style was so popular and prolific. Greek-Revival interiors, especially in the substantial town houses of New York, Boston, and Philadelphia, are epitomized by the double parlor, a pair of nearly identical rooms generally separated by a dividing wall in which was set a wide opening with highly polished sliding mahogany doors. These walls were often ornamented with freestanding columns forming an almost "triumphal arch." When the doors were open, double parlors became essentially one large drawing room for receptions and formal occasions. Both rooms were decorated, carpeted, and furnished more or less identically.

The Greek-Revival style was easily adaptable to popular use by the middle classes, and carpenters and other craftspeople replicated the elements of the style with ease. The development of machine technology during the 1840s made the furniture associated with the style widely available. The side chair on the page opposite is typical of affordable furniture of the day.

A widespread American interest in the Gothic Revival style developed during the 1830s and survived, though with less intensity than at first, throughout much of the nineteenth century. The popularization of this romantic style was due largely to Andrew Jackson Downing (1815-52), a nurseryman and theorist whose book Cottage Residences (1842), as well as subsequent works, disseminated it to the general public. The last of Downing's books, and probably the best known, The Architecture of Country Houses (1850), relied heavily upon the architectural designs of his collaborator, Alexander Jackson Davis (1803-92).[1] In this book, Downing continued to develop ideas about the integration of architecture and the natural setting, ideas that Davis's highly romanticized Gothic-style architectural designs complemented. In the view below, naturalistic and less formalized landscaping is an appropriate setting for what were often rambling houses of irregular plan and profile, placed to take advantage of vistas and views. While Downing and Davis would have termed the house shown here a "villa," they also would have been happy to see a more modest dwelling similarly situated and which, termed a "cottage," they would have seen more appropriately detailed in wood.[2]

13

The Gothic Revival (1835-1850)

THE LADY'S BOUDOIR[3] or sitting room above is glimpsed from a somber and heavy Gothic-style hallway. Within it, colorful chintz, not unlike that used in rooms occupied at this time by Victoria and Albert, loosely slipcover the furniture. The Pugin-inspired wallpaper of gold fleurs-de-lis on a cream-colored background appears at a distance to be almost crosslike in shape, perhaps a clue to the popularity of this particular design. The needlepoint carpet, probably of English manufacture, picks up the color of the green wool Gothic-style window curtains adapted from a plate in Andrew Jackson Downing's *Architecture of Country Houses* (1850).[4] A small Gothic-style center table is covered with a practical baize cloth, while a two-tiered galleried worktable stands next to the main chair and holds knitting and sewing projects. Oak-strip flooring is stained in alternating bands of light and dark wood, probably alluding to the oak-and-walnut floors that even in a wealthy home might have seemed a needless expense. This deceit was common at the time. In contrast, the hallway is cool and somber, as Downing preferred, and is decorated with family busts on marble shafts, and with the typically uncomfortable furniture which seems always to be the special bane of hallways and passages. The chair in the corner carries out the architectural theme of the building without offering any comfort. Pictorial evidence suggests that rooms in even the most consciously Gothic-style homes were usually furnished in a variety of popular styles, with only a few pieces of custom-designed Gothic furniture placed here and there. Only in the greatest Gothic-Revival country houses or in fine town houses where entire rooms were treated in the Gothic style were architects able to design entire suites of furniture to match the room's architecture.[5]

1. *"Kew Gardens Glazed Chintz," from a c. 1850 document, extols the romantic ideals of the mid-nineteenth century. Schumacher.* 2. The Gift: A Christmas and New Year's Present for 1842, *a volume of essays printed in Philadelphia, was bound by S. Moore of that city in a handsome gilded leather cover combining Gothic and Persian motifs.* 3. *"Willement Damask," a textile with a design reminiscent of Elizabethan strapwork. Classic Revivals.* 4. *"Turkey Medallion with Gothic Diaper Ground" is a lush carpet designed in 1829. J. R. Burrows and Company.* 5. *An English stoneware platter with transfer decorations depicting a Gothic castle in a romantic landscape, c. 1840.* 6. *"Ferndale," a rich floral, probably English, c. 1850. Schumacher.* 7. *A boudoir or parlor chair in the Gothic style. Wallpaper background on page 63: "Fleur De Lys," an adaptation of an English paper originally designed by A. W. N. Pugin, c. 1840-1850. Bradbury and Bradbury.*

6

7

THAT AMERICAN families once favored interior decoration of Gothic inspiration is easily explained since nineteenth-century Americans were often inspired by romantic, sentimental notions of the past and with strong revivalistic feelings often associated with the medieval period, especially its ecclesiastical architecture. Much Gothic design originated in England, the source of several of the objects shown on these pages. So pervasive was the Gothic style that most homeowners with any interest in fashion possessed at least a few decorative articles associated with it.

Some idea of the majestic dignity of the New York brownstone row-house blocks built during the 1850s, '60s, and '70s can still be seen in today's New York City.[1] Unified by identical details, fenestration, and bold protruding cornice lines, these brownstone residences were designed in various classical styles, including the Italianate and Second Empire forms, both of which emphasized horizontality and therefore depended upon contiguous row houses of identical styling for the impact of the whole.[2] The houses shown here, all of which are two-bay except for one, are designed along the English terrace scheme, which placed the entrance only a few steps above the sidewalk rather than at the top of a steep flight of stairs. Decidedly less forbidding than their high-stooped counterparts, these dwelling houses present a gracious, welcoming appearance. The houses are further unified by a continuous balcony at the parlor-floor level.

14

Rococo Meets Renaissance (1860-1870)

BY 1870, Rococo-Revival furniture, with its reliance on heavily carved natural forms, was becoming eclipsed by a style known today as "Renaissance Revival."[3] While furniture in this form often incorporated elements of the Rococo style, its forms were becoming much less sensuously curvilinear and florid. As with the fifteenth- and sixteenth-century pieces which served as its inspiration, Renaissance-Revival furniture was more rectilinear in general appearance and more definitely architectural in overall form. Characteristically, furniture designed in this style gloried in the use of incised, paneled decoration, applied mounts of wooden discs sometimes painted black in imitation of ebony, and straight-profiled turned legs rather than the *S*-shaped cabriole legs of Rococo pieces.[4]

The parlor illustrated above is typical of those which appeared in the houses of the upper-middle class just at the time when the Renaissance-Revival style became popular. Though the overall style is definitely mid-century in color and general decoration—including the marble fireplace—the room displays such up-to-date pieces as the matching furniture suite and a rosewood cabinet. The florid carpet, while mid-century in feeling, is decorated with panels which suggest an attempt to control the floral exuberance that generally dominated carpets at the time. The framed areas of tufted wallpaper in a sensuous raspberry hue evoke the satin upholstery characteristic of the period.[5]

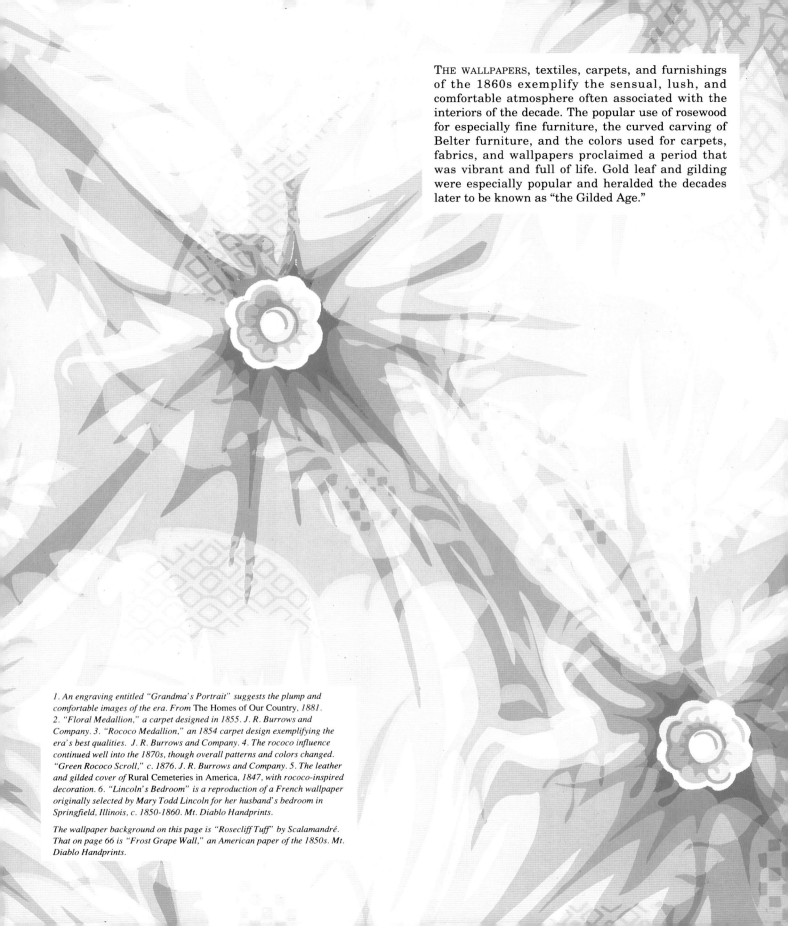

THE WALLPAPERS, textiles, carpets, and furnishings of the 1860s exemplify the sensual, lush, and comfortable atmosphere often associated with the interiors of the decade. The popular use of rosewood for especially fine furniture, the curved carving of Belter furniture, and the colors used for carpets, fabrics, and wallpapers proclaimed a period that was vibrant and full of life. Gold leaf and gilding were especially popular and heralded the decades later to be known as "the Gilded Age."

1. An engraving entitled "Grandma's Portrait" suggests the plump and comfortable images of the era. From The Homes of Our Country, *1881. 2. "Floral Medallion," a carpet designed in 1855. J. R. Burrows and Company. 3. "Rococo Medallion," an 1854 carpet design exemplifying the era's best qualities. J. R. Burrows and Company. 4. The rococo influence continued well into the 1870s, though overall patterns and colors changed. "Green Rococo Scroll," c. 1876. J. R. Burrows and Company. 5. The leather and gilded cover of* Rural Cemeteries in America, *1847, with rococo-inspired decoration. 6. "Lincoln's Bedroom" is a reproduction of a French wallpaper originally selected by Mary Todd Lincoln for her husband's bedroom in Springfield, Illinois, c. 1850-1860. Mt. Diablo Handprints.*

The wallpaper background on this page is "Rosecliff Tuff" by Scalamandré. That on page 66 is "Frost Grape Wall," an American paper of the 1850s. Mt. Diablo Handprints.

The preeminent dwelling built in the the Renaissance Revival style was surely the mansion completed in 1869 for Alexander T. Stewart, which stood on the corner of 34th Street and Fifth Avenue in New York City.[1] A huge fifty-five-room marble pile of essentially symmetrical arrangement, the heavily formal house combined elements of Greek, French, and Italian Renaissance architecture, all of which was topped with a French-inspired mansard roof. Of course, to accommodate more modest budgets, most American houses inspired by this same design ideal were built of wood, a material well suited for transformation into intricate bracketed cornices, balustrades, arcuated elements around doors and windows, and quoins.[2] In New York, as in other major cities, block after block of town houses with Renaissance detailing were constructed. The house shown below, seen from a side street, illustrates a large freestanding residence which has, at its rear, the addition of an art gallery/ballroom and an entrance. A library similar to the one shown on the facing page would likely have been located on the floor behind the bay window. As in most New York town houses, kitchens and service rooms were on the ground or basement-level floor, and servants' rooms were in the attic. By mid-century, dining rooms were usually located on the first or parlor floor.

The Renaissance Revival (1870-1880)

THE ROOM ABOVE represents the typical library in an upper-middle-class home about a decade after the end of the Civil War, one decorated in a conscious and unified form of the Renaissance-Revival style.[3] Since the library was generally the private sitting room of the family, its decoration would have been the most personal of all the public rooms in the house. Family portraits and a wide variety of bric-a-brac with personal associations were considered suitable decorations for such rooms. Chairs, perhaps from an older parlor suite or ones felt to be especially comfortable, are here shown in the typical loose-fitting slipcovers documented in period paintings and photographs.[4] Well-stuffed easy chairs, considered too comfortable for formal parlors, were also increasingly seen in libraries. As always, the ubiquitous center table takes its customary position and functions both as a book table and a writing table well positioned beneath a retractable gas fixture. A number of small tables, placed as needed, include an old teak or rosewood piece used for tea and a gilded metal table of fashionable and recent purchase. A bust of a favorite philosopher or statesman

sits in the bay window where valences in an arabesque design hang beneath wooden cornices constructed to match the room's cabinetry. Atop the bookcases are arranged a collection of small decorative objects which include bronze statues, a bronze urn, and a number of ceramics perhaps collected on a European tour.

The room's most striking decorative feature is the painted decoration on the walls and ceiling. Reflecting the talents of a skilled decorative painter, the designs are stenciled onto the lemon-colored walls in a colorful combination of black, red, various blues, and gilded highlights. "Put together" by a local decorating firm, the room was intended not only for personal comfort, but for show, since libraries were often located—at least in brownstone row houses—as one of a series of rooms opening onto one another through large sliding doors similar to those shown here. Thus, during formal receptions, visitors could stroll through a progression of rooms and then circulate back through the adjoining hallway.

1., 2. Border and field of "Carnation," a carpet designed in 1876. J. R. Burrows and Company. 3. A book cover, 1881, with decoration similar to that often incised on Rennaissance-Revival furniture. 4. "Reform Medallion," a boldly colored carpet, c. 1870. J. R. Burrows and Company. 5. "Tropical Leaves," an 1876 carpet design used in the restoration of Iolani Palace, Honolulu. J. R. Burrows and Company. 6. "Turkey," a carpet designed in 1876. J. R. Burrows and Company. 7. Innovative furniture like this folding chair in the style of George Hunzinger appeared during the period. 8. Touches of gilding and black-painted detailing in imitation of ebony decorate a marble-topped Renaissance-Revival stand. 9. "Henry Ford Panel Stripe," an American wallpaper design, c. 1860-1870. Mt. Diablo Handprints. 10. A French brass mantel clock, c. 1865-1875. 11. "Diamond Stripe," a border paper of French or American origin, c. 1870. Mt. Diablo Handprints. 12. Design for a stenciled wall above wooden paneling from the New York decorating firm of H. D. and J. Moeller, c. 1875. Author's collection. 13. A footrest covered in heavy upholstery fabric or carpet and trimmed with fringe. 14. A Renaissance-Revival armchair in the style of John Jellif of Newark, New Jersey, c. 1870. 15. "Andrew Johnson Suite," c. 1850-1875. Scalamandré.

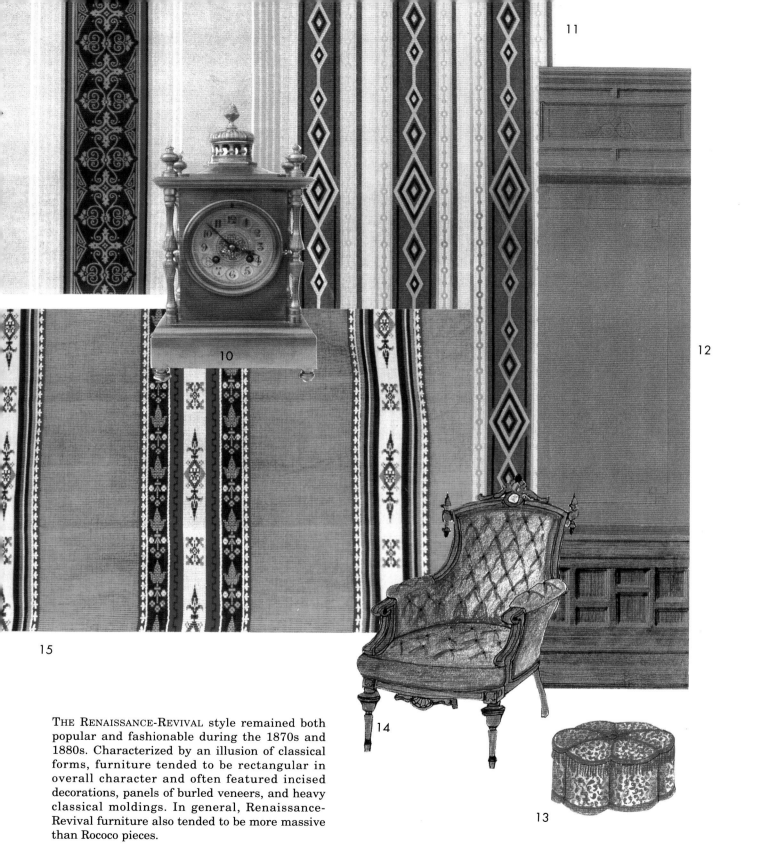

11

12

10

15

14

13

THE RENAISSANCE-REVIVAL style remained both popular and fashionable during the 1870s and 1880s. Characterized by an illusion of classical forms, furniture tended to be rectangular in overall character and often featured incised decorations, panels of burled veneers, and heavy classical moldings. In general, Renaissance-Revival furniture also tended to be more massive than Rococo pieces.

While few houses built during the last quarter of the nineteenth century were exclusively Moorish or Japanese in style or detailing, many did exhibit architectural motifs from Eastern lands. This house, with its Eastern-style dome, window arches, hanging porches, and Chinese-inspired fretwork, is typical in that exotic touches, like much of the rest of Victorian decoration, are applied to the basic Victorian house form. Nothing like this architectural style ever appeared in the Far East, of course, and was, for the most part, a reflection of our particular and unique American experience.

16
The Exotic Craze (1875-1895)

MUCH OF OUR FASCINATION with the late Victorian period lies within its inherent complexity. In America this is particularly evident in buildings and interiors built after the Civil War, a time when the burgeoning economy, a growing sense of national purpose, and the expansion of foreign markets turned the United States into a giant quickly and even frantically moving away from its traditional ties to an agrarian past.[1] No clearer picture of this transition can be found than in the buildings and interiors of the so-called "Gilded Age." [2] Not surprisingly, this fascination with exotic lands and goods found expression within the decoration of houses, and not only those of the well-to-do. For most people the introduction of a few panels of Chinese embroidery, a Middle-Eastern hookah, and a few parasols and paper lanterns was sufficient to transform a room into the new style. For the very rich, of course, there were more options, with the best known and most costly of all, perhaps, being the opulent Japanese parlor decorated by the Herter Brothers

for William H. Vanderbilt at 640 Fifth Avenue in New York.[3] Completed in 1882, the parlor exemplified the triumph of both the professional interior decorator and the period's fascination with exotic objects.[4]

The room shown here suggests the conscious efforts of its occupants to create an oriental room within a typical late Victorian dwelling. In many cases, such interior decoration was undertaken to display a collection of objects gathered during an Eastern tour, as an emblem of fashionable taste, or as a result of exposure to the wonders of exotic and distant lands at one of the fairs and exhibitions popular at the time.[5] Whatever the inspiration, contemporary photographs of fashionable late nineteenth-century interiors usually show several Eastern and oriental objects, though they are frequently scattered among the Renaissance, European, and American antique objects commonly displayed at the time.[6]

1. New and antique Moorish tiles found popular use as fireplace surrounds. 2. A handpainted band of peacock feathers on a wall design from the New York decorating firm of H. D. and J. Moeller, c. 1880. Author's collection. 3. A lacquered bamboo firescreen hung with a piece of silk embroidery.
4. Overstuffed chairs and sofas, upholstered in the "Turkish Style" were a welcome addition to parlors and libraries of the period. 5. Domestically made and decorated ceramics such as vases and plates were often decorated with designs which interpreted oriental, Moorish, and Persian motifs. 6. Light, easily moveable bamboo tables were attractive and useful objects within the exotic interior.
7. Japanese-inspired ceiling papers from the Aesthetic Movement. Bradbury and Bradbury.
8. A decorative element from "Emelita's Frieze," another Aesthetic Movement wallpaper. Bradbury and Bradbury. 9. Simple, inexpensive rush fans, sometimes decorated by the homeowner, were popular and useful decorations. 10. A handpainted frieze of ferns, bamboo, flowers, and butterflies from the New York decorating firm of H. D. and J. Moeller, c. 1880. Author's collection. 11. "Claire's Willow" from the Anglo-Japanese Roomset Series. Bradbury and Bradbury. 12. Inexpensive paper fans can still be easily found and decorated with Asian motifs to provide an authentic period touch to an exotic interior. 13. A student's room, photographed in 1886, showing simple, inexpensive Japanese and Chinese decorative objects. Author's collection. 14. A portion of "Chequerboard" ceiling paper, primarily used as a border. Bradbury and Bradbury. 15. Victorian women spent idle hours painting china "blanks," many decorated with the popular Chinese and Japanese motifs of the period.

Wallpaper background: "Anglo-Japanese Blossom," American, c. 1880s. Original paper in the Cohen House, Oakland, California. Mt. Diablo Handprints.

AS PART of the Aesthetic Movement—which emphasized the importance of art in the design of interiors, particularly in wallpapers, textiles, and other decorative elements—the interest in Moorish, Persian, Egyptian, Indian, and oriental motifs was popularized by many talented designers. Among the best known were the Americans Louis Comfort Tiffany and the Herter Brothers and the Englishmen Owen Jones and Christopher Dresser, who with many others infused the decorative arts of the last quarter of the nineteenth century with a rich and wonderfully colored interpretation of exotic style.

Modestly-scaled houses were quite easily adapted to many, if not all, of the popular late-nineteenth-century architectural styles, and especially to the so-called Queen Anne. Often constructed of wood, like the house above, or of masonry and wood, Queen Anne houses of modest size often boasted the same kinds of architectural features—towers, bays, porches, and complicated woodwork—as their larger counterparts. Tangible expressions of a period of both personal and national confidence,[1] and characterized by a textural richness, both inside and outside, houses of this variety lent themselves especially well to rich colors that emphasized their form, detailing, and visual complexity.

17

Queen Anne in America (1880-1890)

IN HER REMINISCENCE, "A Little Girl's New York," Edith Wharton recalled the Pompeiian-red vestibules characteristic of Manhattan town houses during her post-Civil War childhood.[2] Ever interested in houses, their decoration, and the social mores of her era, Wharton is well known for her dislike of the excessive interior decoration common in late-nineteenth-century America. Preferring French furniture and decorative objects, she probably never selected Pompeiian-red for a vestibule in any home she ever occupied. The popularity of the color's use in entry halls was likely tied to convention and considered a traditional selection at a time when many specific principles of interior decoration were rigidly laid down. The color is warm, rich, and welcoming. Today visitors may see walls painted this rich brick-red at Bullock Hall (c. 1840) in Roswell, Georgia, and at Kingscote (c. 1850-1890), a Gothic-Revival "cottage" in Newport, Rhode Island. Mark Twain's fanciful house in Hartford, Connecticut, also displays a lushly restored entry hall with Pompeiian-red walls and stenciled work originally designed by Louis Comfort Tiffany in 1881.

Living halls were common features in late-nineteenth-century American houses. Influenced in part by the large halls in the medieval English houses that inspired many American homes of the period, these spaces were typically furnished not only as an entryway but also as a parlor or sitting room and invariably contained large, prominent fireplaces. Each of the major first-floor rooms usually opened into the living hall, and from this space the elaborate main staircase rose to the second floor, often ceremoniously. The living hall, as the illustration shows, was often a repository for an odd variety of objects the Victorians took great delight in combining. For example, an eighteenth-century Dutch tall-case clock shares space with a wicker chair, an old Spanish leather-covered armchair, and various oriental porcelains. Family portraits, of which only one is visible here, and several framed photographs also lend a personal note. The walls are decorated with simple stenciling and further embellished with a black fringe at the cornice line. The floor would have been characteristically covered with a large oriental carpet and, in summer, perhaps straw matting.

1. A design for wall decoration by the New York decorating firm of H. D. and J. Mueller, c. 1875-1880. Author's collection. 2. A carpet border called "Aesthetic Medallion," designed in 1889. J. R. Burrows and Company. 3. Partial view of a table top inlaid with various woods and mother of pearl and said to have been purchased in Damascus, c. 1885. 4. An autograph album decorated with exotic motifs, c. 1885. 5. A ceramic fireplace tile, American c. 1890-1900. 6. A stenciled wall design by the firm of H. D. and J. Moeller, c. 1875-1880. 7. "Kelmscott Frieze," adapted by Bradbury and Bradbury from a stencil design by Morris & Company. 8. A small oil painting in a typical late-nineteenth-century frame. Painted by P. Jazet, c. 1879. 9. Pillows made from oriental carpets were appropriate accessories in libraries.

Wallpaper background on this page: "Oxborough Trellis," English, c. 1870-1880. Classic Revivals.

BY THE MID-1880S, when the large wood, brick, and stone houses that most people think of as the epitome of Victorian architecture were in vogue, interior decoration was at its most eclectic. Favored colors were often such rich, deep tones as full-bodied russets, olives, and bottle greens, old golds, deep blues, and browns, each giving credence to the name given the era by Lewis Mumford, "the Brown Decades." Pattern, detail, and exuberant, rich colors characterize many of the period's decorative objects and suggest the phrases often associated with the era— "the Gilded Age," "the Age of Excess." Many of the elements shown here would have been at home in an exotic setting like that shown in the previous chapter.

The celebration of America's centennial in 1876 gave rise to an interest in colonial American architecture and decorative arts. Most of the architecture inspired by the country's colonial past expressed of consequence the most ideal aspects of the earlier work as well as its most picturesque and historically associative elements. Several houses, for example, were built with elements derived from John Hancock's Boston mansion,[1] and others borrowed either the form or architectural features of Washington's Mount Vernon.[2] In all cases, colonial and Federal architectural elements—many of which were confused in the public mind during this period—were juxtaposed within the typical Victorian-era domestic form. This architectural confusion is well illustrated by the house pictured above, where a gambrel roof and colonial-style window sash have been overlayed with a corner bay window and a porch, both hallmarks of the late nineteenth century. Houses like this one would have appeared odd to eighteenth-century Americans, though contemporary Victorians would have seen them ideally as expressions of their historic past.

18

The First Colonial Revival (1885-1900)

MOST HOUSES designed in a recognizable Colonial-Revival style reflect the style externally and internally. This was not always the case at the end of the nineteenth century, when domestic structures designed in one particular style were commonly decorated in various and distinctly different styles on the inside. Colonial-Revival houses, though there were exceptions, generally exhibit stylistic homogeneity because those who commissioned them often had strong feelings for the American past and a conscious aversion to Victorian excess. One of the foremost proponents of the Colonial-Revival style was Arthur Little. Of old New England stock, Little was both an architect and an architectural historian and designed houses that represented some of the most original and academically inspired buildings of their day. Like several of his professional contemporaries, he was also interested in interior design and was responsible for the creation of many noteworthy interiors. The room pictured here takes its inspiration from contemporary photographs of interiors in several houses he designed in the picturesque seaport towns of coastal Massachusetts. In several of these photographs, flowered chintz is used not only on furniture but as wallcovering, a surprising and fresh approach for the period. One wonders whether Little's friendship with designer Ogden Codman may

have inspired his use of these colorful cottons.

In the sitting room above, some of the nineteenth century's love of eclectic furniture is still evidenced, especially in the use of the wicker lounge and the "layered" assemblage of decorative objects. Touches of an antiquarian interest and a simplification of form and line, however, suggest the advent of a new interior style, a newness reflected in the use of white paint on the paneling. Antiques were sought out with a renewed interest, and reproduced or adapted furniture and objects were readily available. for purchase. Floor covering would have included room-sized oriental carpets in winter and straw matting strewn with small oriental rugs in summer. Evoking the American past and the ideals of the American home, Colonial-Revival architecture is intended to be charming and cozy and generally emphasizes the symbolic image of the hearth. In the sitting room above, the late-nineteenth-century inglenook, or cozy alcove before the fireplace, becomes a vivid symbol of hearth and home, its built-in white-painted bench, reminiscent of an old kitchen settle, offering a deep seat and a place to read or chat with friends.

William Morris (1834-1896) used his considerable talents not only for the design of wallpapers and textiles, but also for carpets. His own personal carpet collection included many fine eastern examples, and it was from them, as well as the landscape around him, that the designer drew much of his inspiration. Though Morris designed and produced hand-knotted carpets, beginning in the late 1870s he also designed carpets that were produced on machines by professional carpet-making firms. Since these were far less costly than the hand-knotted carpets, demand was great. These carpets were especially popular in the United States, particularly the sturdy Kidderminsters.

"Tulip and Lily," said to be among the best known of Morris's carpet designs, is shown above as a runner and would be effective in a hallway or stairway. The carpet, which is woven on antique looms in England by Woodward Grosvenor & Co. Ltd., is also produced in a worsted Wilton carpet suitable for wall-to-wall or fitted installation. J. R. Burrows and Company.

The wallpaper and textile designs of William Morris were in many respects strikingly revolutionary in appearance, especially when compared with the exuberant floral designs they replaced. Decidedly naturalistic and beautifully colored, Morris's designs reflected many of the ideas of the English Arts and Crafts Movement, of which he was a major spokesman. Strongly influenced by the natural setting around him, Morris interpreted nature in a stylized, two dimensional manner that is instantly recognizable. Morris's wallpapers and textiles became increasingly popular in the United States after the late 1870s and were used in many homes, among them the then rather avant-garde stone mansion designed by the architect H. H. Richardson in 1885 for the Glessner family of Chicago. Of particular interest is one period photograph of a bedroom in the Glessner House that shows several of Morris's patterns used simultaneously in the same space. The bedroom walls were papered with the pattern called "Sunflower," the windows curtained with "Rose and Thistle" chintz (c. 1882), and a nearby chair covered with "African Marigold" (c. 1876).

The paper shown above, "Willow Bough Minor," is one of Morris's best-known and most endearing designs. Like his carpet designs, Morris's wallpaper and textile designs are appropriate for use in American Colonial-Revival interiors of the late nineteenth century, not only because of historic precedents for their use, but also because of their intrinsic charm. The example above is machine-printed and is available through Arthur Sanderson and Sons. Sanderson owns the original pearwood blocks used for Morris's papers and still uses them in the production of the firm's hand-printed papers. Several patterns are available as machine-printed papers.

In Berkeley, California, at the end of the nineteenth century, urban sprawl and development had become of great concern to local citizens. One improvement society, the Hillside Club, was especially concerned with the area's natural charms and set guidelines for the preservation of the landscape and for the design and development of the town. The result was a unique group of wood-framed shingled houses in a style now termed "Bay Area Rustic," [1] houses that are "rustic, picturesque, commodious, unobtrusive, . . . respecting the setting and reflecting the moralistic attitude of life." [2] Bernard Maybeck, a local resident and architect, agreed with these precepts and was probably best known for the private houses and public buildings he designed along these principles. [3] In nearby San Francisco, and throughout the region, architects such as Julia Morgan, Ernest Coxhead, Albert Farr, and Edgar Mathews [4] built residences like those above in a shingled style that mirrored the Berkeley examples and those of the English Arts and Crafts movement in their simple, honest construction. [5]

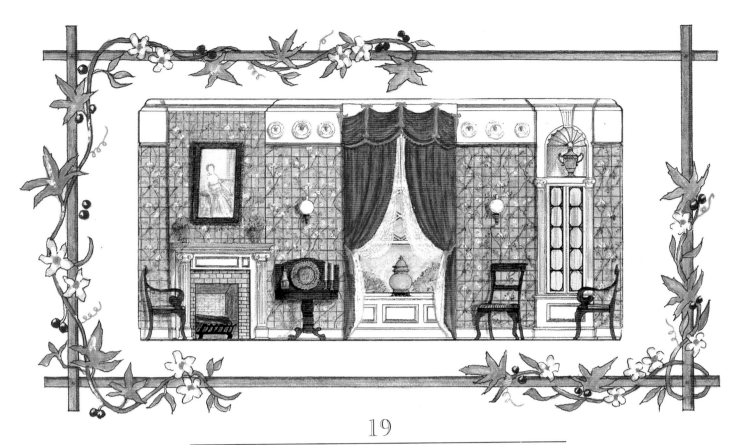

19
Bay Area Rustic/Classical (1895-1900)

NOT EVERY rustic-style house built in the San Francisco Bay area at the end of the nineteenth century had corresponding rustic-style interiors. While many did indeed have interiors finished with simple unstained or unvarnished redwood sheathing and well-crafted exposed structural work,[6] others were characterized by natural redwood carved into classically inspired architectural forms.[7] Still others, and particularly those built for San Francisco's more fashionable citizens, featured interiors with *painted* classical detailing. The Russell Osborn House in San Francisco exemplifies this third variety. Designed by Ernest Coxhead in 1896, the house, which is still extant, presents from the street a rustic facade that quite belies the classically detailed interior behind its modest front door. Perhaps the only hint of classicism behind the dark shake walls are the minimal classical features surrounding the door and windows, a treatment totally unlike the house's Colonial-Revival contemporaries, where the architectural detailing tends to crowd the facade. Bay Area rustics are closely linked with the design tenets of the English Arts and Crafts movement—which emphasized the indigenous beauty of materials, the honest use of materials, and rustic simplicity—and may be considered "an impressive prelude to the Arts and Crafts movement in American architecture."[8] The room above imparts the sense of gentility and formality so appealing to established San Franciscans a century ago and hints at the presence of a professional decorator, particularly in the curtains which are anything but simple and have been chosen to complement the wallpaper. Late-nineteenth-century decorators emphasized the treatment of curtains, and the design and fabrication of them was a major part of many decorating businesses. Reproductions of early-nineteenth-century furniture, rather than antique pieces, appear at the room's perimeter and would have included a dining table with a base similar to that of the small table against the wall. The floor covering would probably have been an oriental carpet or one of solid or subtle coloring chosen to complement the wallpaper.

1. A sterling-silver candy dish of Art Nouveau design, c. 1910. 2. "Wren's Nest Study," an American wallpaper made in 1897. Mt. Diablo Handprints. 3. "Chrystanthemum," a carpet designed in 1890. J. R. Burrows and Company. 4., 5. Alternate colorways of "Billings Acanthus," an American wallpaper, c. 1890-1900. The document color appears as the background of page 87. Mt. Diablo Handprints. 6. The author's great-aunt, New York, 1909. The sitter's dress reflects an emphasis upon simpler clothing design.

Wallpaper background on this page: "Hummingbird Lattice," a reproduction of a French paper, c. 1900-1910. Mt. Diablo Handprints.

LUSH NATURALISTIC motifs seem especially appropriate for use in the classic interiors of houses built in a region known for its spectacular surroundings. The Art-Nouveau style, which is characterized by sensuous, elongated, flowing, and intertwining natural forms, was current at the same time that Bay Area Rustic houses were first being built and is particularly suitable for their interiors.

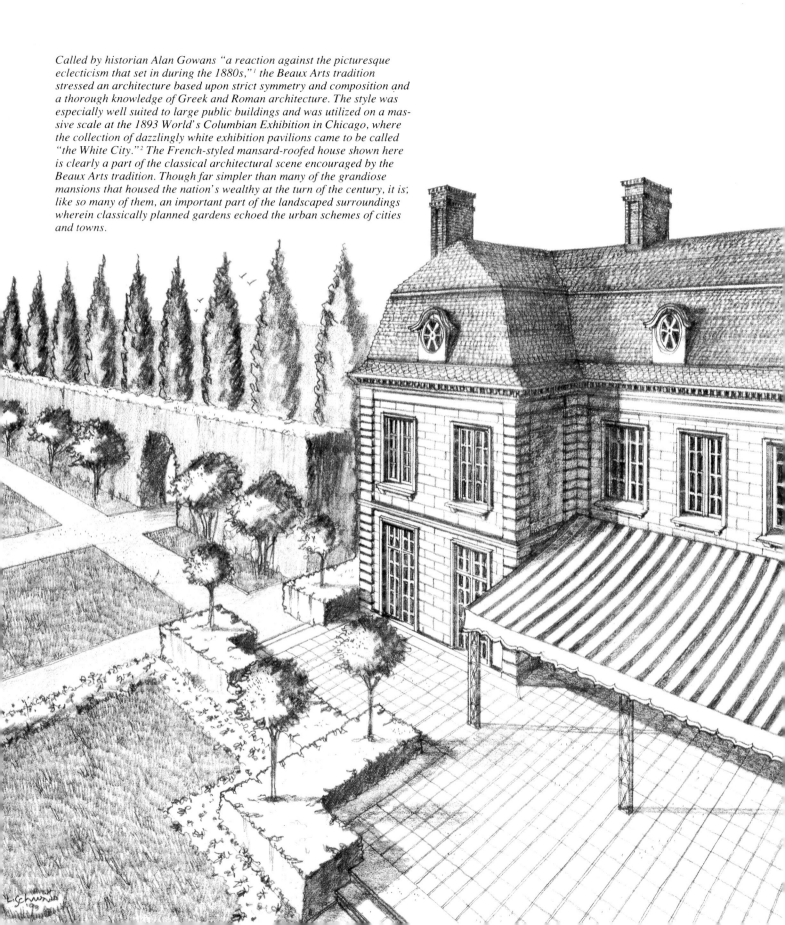

Called by historian Alan Gowans *"a reaction against the picturesque eclecticism that set in during the 1880s,"*[1] the Beaux Arts tradition stressed an architecture based upon strict symmetry and composition and a thorough knowledge of Greek and Roman architecture. The style was especially well suited to large public buildings and was utilized on a massive scale at the 1893 World's Columbian Exhibition in Chicago, where the collection of dazzlingly white exhibition pavilions came to be called *"the White City."*[2] The French-styled mansard-roofed house shown here is clearly a part of the classical architectural scene encouraged by the Beaux Arts tradition. Though far simpler than many of the grandiose mansions that housed the nation's wealthy at the turn of the century, it is, like so many of them, an important part of the landscaped surroundings wherein classically planned gardens echoed the urban schemes of cities and towns.

20
Design Advice for the Elite (1900-1920)

WHEREAS architects and professional upholsterers were largely responsible for interior decoration during the eighteenth and nineteenth centuries, by the early years of the twentieth professional interior decorators were generally involved with work within the walls of a building. Perhaps the best known of these decorators were Ogden Codman and Elsie de Wolfe, both of whom championed a style that was restrained, classic, and, in comparison with most late-nineteenth-century interior design, quite simple and chaste. Codman is best remembered today for the book he co-wrote with Edith Wharton who, though not a professional decorator, was intensely interested in the subject. Entitled *The Decoration of Houses* (1897), their book became a veritable handbook of correct and tasteful interior decoration and is still in print today. Intended for the owners and decorators of large houses, the book provides interesting insights into the tastes of both authors as well as of their elite audience.

The illustration above suggests a small sitting room designed in a style that Codman, Wharton, and de Wolfe would have favored. The room's character is derived primarily from its architectural features, which include pale gray painted paneling or *boiserie* and a marble mantelpiece and white-painted overmantel with gilded decoration. Especially typical of Codman's and Wharton's taste is the furniture, which includes reproductions of white-painted Louis XVI-style armchairs, covered in chintz, as well as small marquetry tables. A folding screen, covered in gold-covered silk, stands in a corner and echoes the spirit and richness of the restrained gilded objects. Carpeting in a room of this style could have included several options. If the floor were of an especially handsome parquet, it might have been left bare. More likely, it would have been covered with a costly French carpet in either an Aubusson or Savonnerie style or even with an oriental-style carpet of the kind pictured in several of Wharton's rooms.[3] Solid-colored carpets of rich, dark reds or bronze-colored velvets were also popular at the time.

1

2

1. "Ogden's Floral," a fabric and matching wallpaper epitomizing Ogden
Codman's and Edith Wharton's preference for light printed cotton fabrics.
Schumacher. 2. Codman and Wharton were especially partial to cotton toiles of
French design and manufacture. This printed toile of plum on antique white is
typical of the lively fabrics which replaced heavy silks and brocades in many of
their interiors. 3. "Worthington," a crisp and colorful cotton, is derived from the
silk brocades of Philippe La Salle in the late eighteenth century. This glazed
chintz would surely have been a favorite of Codman, Wharton, and Elsie de
Wolfe. Schumacher. 4. Codman and Elsie de Wolfe used pedestals similar to
these in a project they designed jointly in New York City in 1910. 5. Codman
used fine reproductions of eighteenth-century French and English antiques in
most of his interiors. This Louis XVI open armchair is covered in a pink and
white striped silk.

3

4

5

THE FABRICS on these facing pages, some of which were also used as wallcoverings, are of the styles and types that appealed to Ogden Codman, Edith Wharton, and Elsie de Wolfe at the beginning of the twentieth century. Together with the furniture and other objects shown here, all are a departure from the heavy, ponderous decorative items that were common during the last two decades of the nineteenth century. All suggest the designers' preferences for fine furniture and decorative objects of French design. The "Brown Decades" have clearly given way to clear, fresh colors, graceful lines, and elegant forms.

Design Advice for the Elite 91

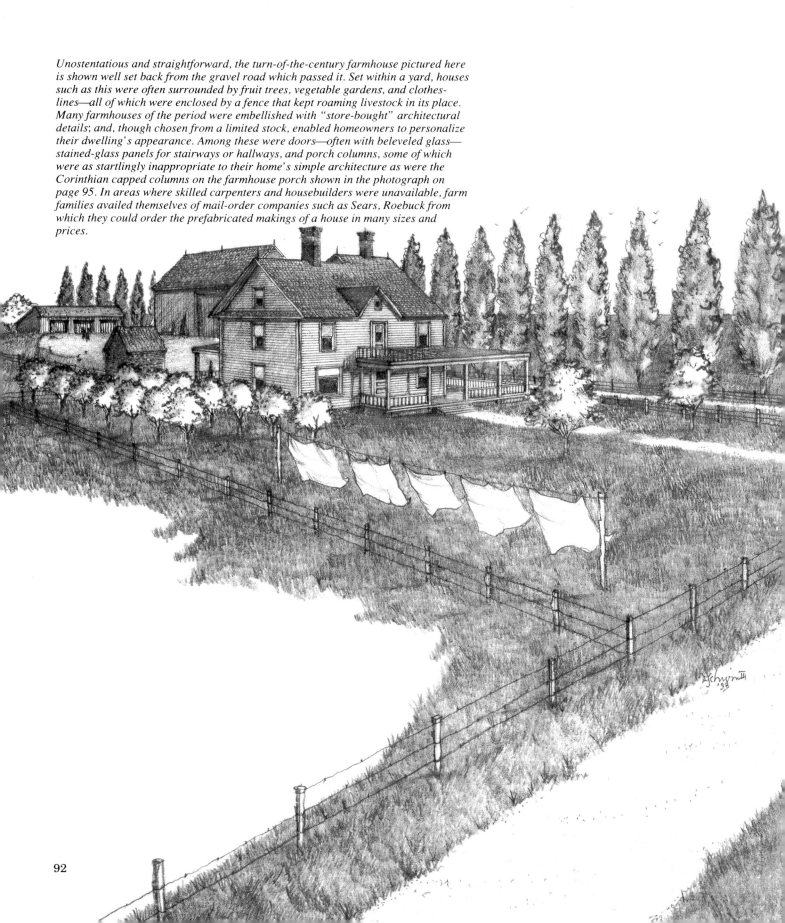

Unostentatious and straightforward, the turn-of-the-century farmhouse pictured here is shown well set back from the gravel road which passed it. Set within a yard, houses such as this were often surrounded by fruit trees, vegetable gardens, and clothes-lines—all of which were enclosed by a fence that kept roaming livestock in its place. Many farmhouses of the period were embellished with "store-bought" architectural details; and, though chosen from a limited stock, enabled homeowners to personalize their dwelling's appearance. Among these were doors—often with beleveled glass—stained-glass panels for stairways or hallways, and porch columns, some of which were as startlingly inappropriate to their home's simple architecture as were the Corinthian capped columns on the farmhouse porch shown in the photograph on page 95. In areas where skilled carpenters and housebuilders were unavailable, farm families availed themselves of mail-order companies such as Sears, Roebuck from which they could order the prefabricated makings of a house in many sizes and prices.

21
_____

Home Sweet Home (1895-1910)

FOR THE FARMERS, ranchers, and many others who lived and worked away from urban centers where the major household goods could be procured, mail-order companies were essential to the outfitting and decoration of homes. Sears, Roebuck and Company was, of course, the best known and was responsible for the furnishing of thousands of American farm and ranch houses during the late-nineteenth and early-twentieth centuries. Since few working-class people earned more than a dollar a day, such inexpensive 1897 prices as 34¢ for a chair or $4.00 for a rocker were not really as cheap as they seem.[1] A brass bed at $42.50, or a parlor suite with art nouveau decoration at $47.00, would have been a once-in-a-lifetime purchase. Of particular note in the 1897 Sears catalog are the upholstery fabrics for the latter, which include crushed plush in assorted colors, cotton tapestry, brocatelle, a material called brocaline, and silk and satin damasks. Genuine leather is also listed for use on upholstered rockers and easy chairs. Couches, a term used for a kind of sofa bed or lounge similar to the one in the illustration above, were available in numerous coverings and in imported corduroy. Wallpapers had to be selected without benefit of colored pictures, but Sears would send samples upon request. Among the most common papers appear to have been those printed on white backgrounds with designs of scrolls, stripes, geometrics, and florals. These cost 24¢ per double roll and are described as including "the new blues, greens,

lilacs, reds, tans, and terra cottas." The catalog also mentions the availability of blended border papers, noting that they are "the latest novelty." These papers apparently grade the colors in the background paper so that the lightest shade is at the ceiling. Embossed papers and leatherettes are also stocked, though considerably more costly at 50¢ per double roll.

In the room above, simple catalog-purchased furniture is shown in the parlor of a farmhouse in the early twentieth century. A safe, indispensable in the homes of prosperous farming families, is shown decorously covered with a cloth, as is the easy chair in the bay window. Photographs of family members, highlighted with pastels as an alternative to the costly oil portraits in well-to-do households, hang close to the ceiling in elaborate parlor frames, together with a gilt-framed pastoral scene. By this date, furniture and room settings still displayed upholstery styles and furniture forms of the Victorian era. Also popular, however, were the emerging Art Nouveau and Mission styles, both of which could be purchased inexpensively. The emphasis, though on comfort, was also very much on a perceived idea of style—and especially that which was suggested by gilt decoration and the illusion of costliness. The room is shown in the colder months, with draperies and portieres in place.

1. *An immigrant farm couple on their wedding day, c. 1905. 2. A cut-glass oil cruet, c. 1900. 3. Parlor suites generally included a settee similar to this one and two open-armed chairs. 4. Tables were usually placed at the center of parlors. 5. Perhaps made as a gift, this fanciful wooden piece is inscribed "Mizpah," a biblical parting salutation used in modern times as a talisman. 6. A carnival glass mug, 1911. 7. A sampler made by the author's paternal grandmother while a schoolgirl. Alsace, c. 1899. 8. An American cabinet clock, known to collectors as a "parlor walnut" because of its usual location in the home, c. 1890. 9. A parlor rocker cost about $4.00 in 1897. 10. Three generations of an American farm family before their new house, c. 1900. 11. Plushes and crushed velvets found fashionable use as upholstery on parlor furniture. 12. One of a number of recipes bought to America by the author's paternal grandmother, c. 1900. 13. China was invariably decorated with floral motifs and lots of gold.*

Wallpaper background on this page: "Passion Flower," a French design, c. 1900-1910. Mt. Diablo Handprints. Wallpaper background on page 95: "Wren's Nest," American basket-weave design, c. 1910. Mt. Diablo Handprints.

THE MODERATELY priced articles illustrated here would have been familiar to most farm families in the opening decades of the twentieth century. Most farm families knew the realities of hard work and valued the household objects which took so long to acquire. For many who had left Europe with few personal possessions, the accumulation of items such as these was an important part of establishing roots in a new land.

While the presence of porches on houses suggests a leisurely life style, or at least the aspiration for one, these exterior spaces have been important features on even the humblest American dwellings for centuries. Although most prevalent from the middle of the nineteenth century, porches did exist on houses before this date, though certainly not as frequently as they did later on. The most famous American porch of all, of course, is the one that George Washington conceived for Mount Vernon at the end of the eighteenth century. By the 1880s and '90s, perhaps the golden age of the American porch (or "verandah" or "Piazza," as porches were frequently called), houses often boasted exuberant combinations of covered and open exterior spaces, both kinds to an increasing degree related to the interior spaces which adjoined them. In the drawing below, a covered porch connects with a terrace and thence to a conservatory—later called a sunroom—giving the house's occupants several options for the enjoyment of the out-of-doors in various weather conditions.

22

Porches, Piazzas, and Sunrooms (c. 1875-1930)

BEFORE THE ELECTRIC FAN and the air conditioner was the porch. A commonly seen part of American houses during the 1840s and '50s, the porch was an indispensable feature of even the most modest cottages by the 1870s. Large houses, of course, generally had several, and, in most instances, their location, exposure, and relationship to adjoining interior spaces determined how they were used. Those which faced the street were the most public, their use requiring proper dress and decorous behavior. The largest houses often had private and secluded porches and verandahs opening off private family rooms and bedrooms and facing away from public view. Servants often enjoyed porches designated for their own use. These were logically off service wings and situated away from family view. Period photographs reveal many late-nineteenth-century porches to have been furnished with surprising opulence, particularly when well protected from rain or when able to be enclosed with glass sash during cooler months. Several photographs show oriental carpets on the floors and a profusion of easily moveable furniture, much of it naturally colored wicker arranged in small groups as needed. With the interest in classical and Beaux-Arts architectural styles among the rich at century's end, porches were suitably "translated" into loggias and galleries. The loggia pictured above suggests the kind of "outside room" popular among the well-to-do and commonly found at their countryseats.

In the view above, latticework covers the walls, giving the illusion of an elegant outdoor setting. Popularized by decorator Elsie de Wolfe, who used it to great effect in the dining room at the Colony Club in New York in 1907, latticework was often painted green and placed in front of gray-painted walls. De Wolfe recommended trailing ivy on the trellis and a playing fountain placed against a wall.

AMERICANS have always enjoyed areas devoted to casual relaxation and fresh air. The Victorians were known for their architectural use of the porch but perhaps less so for their equal love of glassed-in conservatories and verandas. Early in the twentieth century, many homes featured sun parlors, sun porches, or rooms located at the eastern or southern side of the house designed to catch the sun. As the century progressed, outdoor terraces and patios signaled a change in life style and the kinds of furnishings and objects used in these areas of leisure.

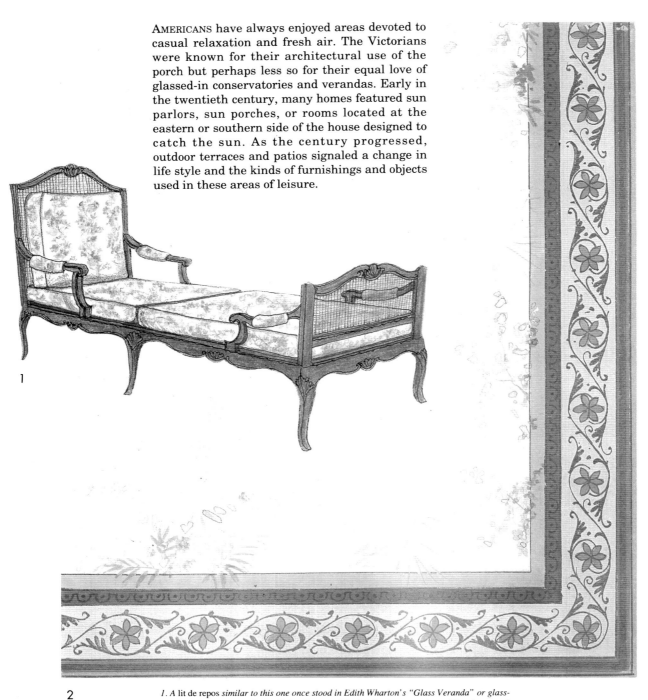

1. *A lit de repos similar to this one once stood in Edith Wharton's "Glass Veranda" or glass-enclosed porch at "Land's End," her Newport, Rhode Island, summer home. The piece was later moved to her library at "The Mount" in Lenox, Massachusetts, after 1901. 2. This partial design for a ceiling suggests lush ferns and pastel flowers against a very pale blue sky. Although it was never executed, Ogden Codman designed a Pompeiian-style ceiling for Wharton's "Glass Veranda," complete with floral roping, clouds, and blue sky. Ceiling illustration, c. 1875-1885, from the New York decorating firm of H. D. and J. Moeller. Author's collection.*

3. *This lush fabric in autumnal colors is probably best known for its use in the family quarters at the White House during the Truman and Eisenhower years. Photographs from the early 1950s indicate that it served as furniture slipcovers in the wide third-floor sitting room. Of English design, it first appeared c. 1940 and is now part of Schumacher's Centennial Collection. Its coloring and pattern suggest its suitablity for use in a garden or sun room furnished in a mid-twentieth-century fashion. One can easily see it covering cushions and chair backs of the type of bamboo furniture popular in garden rooms of the 1950s and '60s.*

3

4. *A lively pattern of brightly colored stylized flowers and leaves sets a striking note against the dark-blue background of this fabric from the author's collection. Probably American and dating from the 1930s or '40s, this cotton fabric by an unknown maker is typical of inexpensive goods that middle-class householders bought for use as tablecloths, aprons, kitchen curtains, and porch-furniture cushions.*

4

With the growing prosperity of the working and middle classes, the need for inexpensive housing was keenly felt by the
beginning of the twentieth century. Responding to the need,
Gustav Stickley published a magazine called The Craftsman
(1901-16) that featured, for the most part, simple, modestly
scaled houses. Designed largely for young middle-class couples with progressive ideas and a predilection for an informal
life style, these bungalows, as they were sometimes called,
responded to young Americans' needs in ways that the architecture of the previous century had not.[1] Wood, textured con-
crete and stucco, and rough-faced bricks or boulders were
favorite exterior treatments. Most Craftsman houses, and
even the most modest, such as that seen here, had porches or
unroofed terraces and, in warmer climates, vine-covered per-
golas that extended living spaces to the out-of-doors.

23

The Craftsman Era (c. 1905-1920)

ANDREW JACKSON DOWNING'S 1850 demand for truthfulness in architecture became a battle cry by century's end and was echoed years later in Frank Lloyd Wright's call for a new architectural integrity where brick was brick, steel was steel, and glass was glass.[2] With much the same spirit as Downing, Gustav Stickley (1857-1942), a contemporary of Wright's, created furniture and decorative objects and espoused an architecture based on simplicity of form and honesty of materials. His design credo was the creation of furniture that, in his words, would be "fitted for the place it was to occupy and the work it had to do, [furniture that was] comfortable, durable, and easy to take care of."[3] As the living room above suggests, the general character of the Craftsman interior was one of modest, homey comfort. As Stickley wrote, "in creating a home atmosphere, the thing that pays and pays well is honesty. A house should be the outward and visible expression of the life, work, and thought of its inmates. In its planning and furnishing, the station in life of the owner should be expressed in a dignified manner, not disguised."[4] The room shown is characteristic of the modest Craftsman-style bungalow. Among its typical elements are the partially paneled walls, the tile-fronted fireplace, and the broad cased openings between rooms. The ceiling beams and the wooden floor are further features that provide a natural-appearing envelope within which color and textures, carefully chosen, reenforce the particular environment favored by Stickley. His own living room, was described by the designer as reminiscent of a forest, "brown and green with the glint of sunshine through the leaves, suggested by the gold of the windows and the gleam of copper in the hearth-hoods, the door latches, and the vases and bowls on the bookcases and table."[5] Surprising, perhaps, is the presence of the rattan chair in this interior scene. In order to counter the criticism that too much of his Craftsman furniture made rooms too monotonous, Stickley introduced a line of willow chairs and settees provided with finishes of brown or one that gave the impression of green. These pieces, along with softly colored fabrics of textured linen, natural-colored flax, or dull-finished linen made these interiors anything but monotonous. Indeed, some of Stickley's names for colors he favored impart an atmospheric feeling about interior spaces in the Craftsman style. For example, he used such adjectives as "wood," "sunny," "rusty," and "damp" to describe brown, yellow, pine-needle green, and grass green respectively.[6]

1. "Honeysuckle," an English wallpaper, c. 1900-1920, reflects the lingering Art Nouveau style popular during this period. Bradbury and Bradbury. 2. Ceramic vase with a forest-green glaze. 3. Hand-painted ornamental borders. Top: "Oakhurst." Bottom: "Poppy Border." PY-WE-ACK Studio. 4. Bradbury and Bradbury's reproduction of "Thistle," an English wallpaper, c. 1900-1920. 5. Vase with chrysanthemum design and turqoise glaze, c. 1910-1920. 6. "Riverside," a wallpaper frieze of period design by Carol Mead. 7. Oak armchair with reclining back and leather cushions, c. 1910. 8. Oak lady's desk, c. 1910. 9. Portion of "Wild Rose," a wallpaper border by Carol Mead. 10. Porcelain plate, c. 1910. 11. Roseville Pottery bowl (pattern no. 473-6), American, c. 1920. 12. Plant stands could be easily made by following printed patterns. 13. A reproduction of an English carpet called "Mildenhall," c. 1900. J. R. Burrows and Company. 14. Hand-painted ornamental borders from PY-WE-ACK Studio. Top: "Arroyo Ginkgo." Bottom: "Liberty Rose." 15. A door handle by Gustav Stickley, c. 1910. Wallpaper background on page 103: "Bower," English, c. 1910, reproduced by Bradbury and Bradbury.

CRAFTSMAN-STYLE homes were intended to be comfortable, natural in appearance, and—ideally—furnished and appointed with well-crafted handmade objects. But many factory-made items of the period were acceptable furnishings and allowed homeowners across America to follow the principles set out by Gustav Stickley.

With special appeal on the West Coast and in Florida, where the Spanish had their earliest footholds, the Spanish Revival style had particular force during the 1920s and '30s. In California, where the fledgling movie industry created stars with a need for appropriate housing, the Spanish style was especially in vogue.[1] The same was true in Florida, particularly in the resort communities where the well-to-do found the inner-courtyard style well-suited to their leisurely wintertime pursuits and a novel change from their neoclassical estates in the North.[2] While the style was often used on major domestic buildings, it was well-adapted to the small residential structures of the middle classes and to the ideals expressed in the popular bungalow styles.[3]

24
The Spanish Revivals (1910-1930)

THERE WERE THREE major variations of the Spanish-Revival style. Though all share in the same tradition, each is quite different from the other. The first is the most literal and the rarest because it occurred almost exclusively in the geographic region from which it drew its inspiration. Designed around patios or courts and called "Southwestern Style" or "Spanish-Colonial Revival," it had strong architectural associations with historic examples and often employed traditional techniques and materials in its construction. The second variation is best seen in expensively furnished Palm Beach mansions, popularly called "Mediterranean villas" but largely inspired by antique Spanish and Moorish buildings. The third variation, the most familiar, is seen above. Built for middle-class families as a response to the grander versions only the wealthy could afford, these modestly scaled versions were popular in Florida and California, where the style was especially appropriate. Many were inspired by the design of affordable bungalows and were Spanish in appearance only in their exterior style and a few interior features. Few were centered around inner patios or courts like the first variation, and fewer still utilized costly antique artifacts or even reproductions of architectural elements like the second. Floor plans were chacteristically utilitarian, and rooms were often located on one floor.[4] In such a modest setting as that seen here, interior decoration in the Spanish style was often limited to a variety of inexpensive accessories such as lamps, curtain rods, and ironwork railings andirons. Mass-produced vaguely Spanish-appearing Grand Rapids furniture was readily available. Here the architecture is largely responsible for imparting a Spanish atmosphere, while the furniture and fabrics are simply generic. The pale pink color on the wall seems almost integral with the white painted plaster walls at the fireplace and in the adjoining hallway. A tiled floor is suggested in the entry hall and tiles cover the hearth.

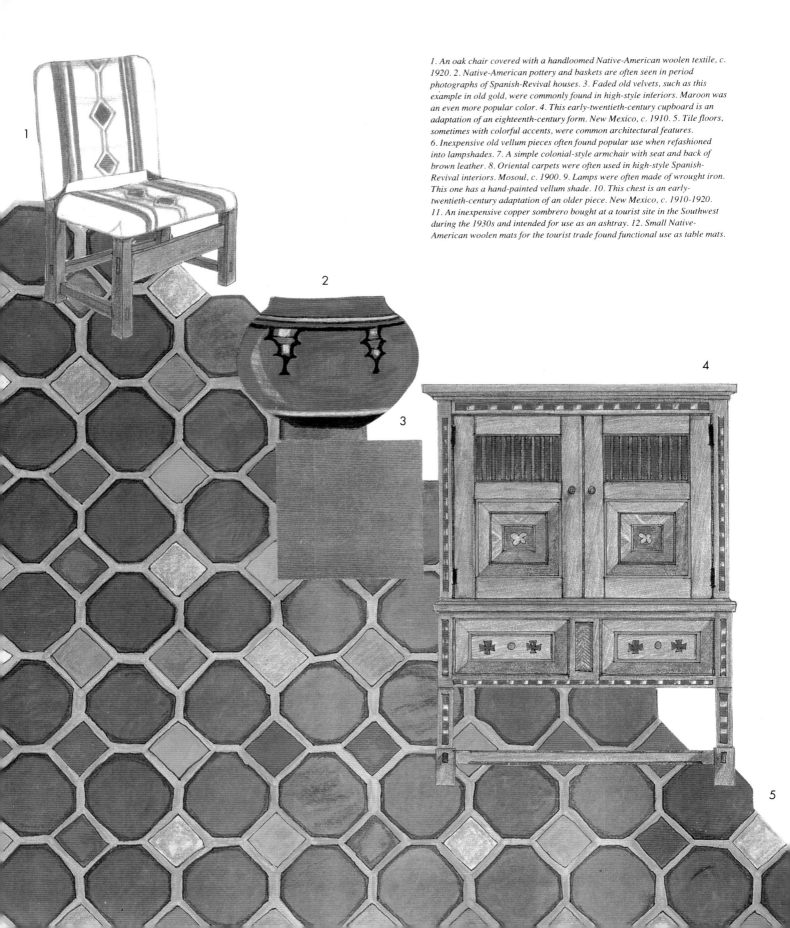

1. An oak chair covered with a handloomed Native-American woolen textile, c. 1920. 2. Native-American pottery and baskets are often seen in period photographs of Spanish-Revival houses. 3. Faded old velvets, such as this example in old gold, were commonly found in high-style interiors. Maroon was an even more popular color. 4. This early-twentieth-century cupboard is an adaptation of an eighteenth-century form. New Mexico, c. 1910. 5. Tile floors, sometimes with colorful accents, were common architectural features. 6. Inexpensive old vellum pieces often found popular use when refashioned into lampshades. 7. A simple colonial-style armchair with seat and back of brown leather. 8. Oriental carpets were often used in high-style Spanish-Revival interiors. Mosoul, c. 1900. 9. Lamps were often made of wrought iron. This one has a hand-painted vellum shade. 10. This chest is an early-twentieth-century adaptation of an older piece. New Mexico, c. 1910-1920. 11. An inexpensive copper sombrero bought at a tourist site in the Southwest during the 1930s and intended for use as an ashtray. 12. Small Native-American woolen mats for the tourist trade found functional use as table mats.

MIDDLE-CLASS families, especially those living in Florida and California during the heyday of the Spanish Revival, could purchase numbers of appropriate accessories for their homes. Since the houses of the wealthy and the notable, particularly movie stars and Palm Beach socialites, were a major inspiration, many inexpensive reproductions and artful adaptations were similar, at least stylistically, with the antiques and costly reproductions found in larger homes.

The Spanish Revivals 107

Houses like the one above appeared in American suburbs with increasing regularity during the early decades of the twentieth century. Indebted in many respects to the Queen Anne style of the previous century, many of which displayed half-timbered elements and similar rambling floor plans, Tudor-style houses also appealed to similar feelings of heritage and a connection to an earlier English tradition engendered by British Queen Anne counterparts. Of course, modestly scaled "Banker Tudor" houses appeared in many suburban areas, where the style was especially popular.[1]

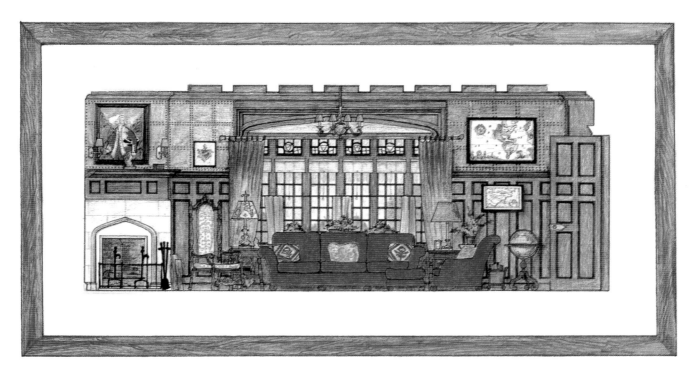

25
Bankers' Tudor (c. 1910-1930)

PERHAPS ABOVE ALL ELSE, the English Tudor style was seen as picturesque and comforting and, to many, a fitting setting in which to play out lives centered around a perception of Anglo-Saxon privilege and prestige. During the early decades of the twentieth century, in fact, the style was as popular as the Colonial Revival and was widely used in domestic buildings throughout America.

The library pictured above represents the quintessential room in the American Tudor-style house. More than any other interior space, the Tudor library seems the very embodiment of heritage, intellect, established comfort, and leisure. Paneled in oak that may have been colored and distressed to give it the patina of age, the room is also characterized by a stone-faced fireplace with Tudor arch, a beamed ceiling, and a bay window in which the glass in the window transoms has been decorated with heraldic motifs. Although all architectural objects here seem to have been especially fabricated for the space, it was not uncommon, especially in the largest examples of the style, to find that artifacts and sometimes even entire rooms had been re-created from European buildings. Well-to-do collectors purchased suitable antique furniture from dealers, but were also able to select excellent reproductions suitable for use in these rooms. Of particular note above is the leather

wallcovering, held in place by an arrangement of decorative tacks. Upon the walls are hung an ancestral portrait—or one intended to appear as such—a framed coat of arms, and two framed antique maps which suggest a larger collection hanging elsewhere in the room. Bookcases, the end of one of which is partially visible behind the open door, likely hold a variety of leather-bound books and possibly a special collection related to a particular subject—perhaps a collection of Shakespeare, English medieval history, or cartography.

Befitting a masculine room, the furnishings include a well-upholstered sofa and matching chair covered in claret-colored valvet and a reproduction of a seventeenth-century walnut armchair covered in a tone-on-tone voided valvet. Damask-covered pillows in a bold Renaissance-style pattern add a touch of sumptuousness to the upholstered furniture. At the windows, simple moss-green velvet curtains hang from a bronze-finished pole. Utilitarian linen curtains and ecru-colored shades provide the necessary sun control. A hardwood floor, which might be decorated along its perimeter with a contrasting parquet border, would likely have been covered with an oriental carpet, perhaps an old Shirvan, Feraghan, or Herat, or a solid-colored modern carpet of moss-green or claret-colored wool.

1. Reproductions of sixteenth- and seventeenth-century furniture and architectural features were readily available during the early twentieth century. This modern reproduction of a seventeenth-century English chair covered in leather is made by Heart of the Wood. 2. The well-to-do often collected maps as accessories for their libraries. This one shows the United States, c. 1830. 3. This woolen tapestry fabric was intended for upholstery and was made between 1910 and 1915. The example shown is the original document from the Schumacher Archives. 4. Old vellum pieces such as this page from a Latin song book were abundant and inexpensive at the time and were often fashioned into lampshades. 5. "Lion and Dove" is a wallpaper frieze reproduced from a 1900 English design by Walter Crane. Bradbury and Bradbury. 6. "Gobelin's Forest" is a fabric inspired by a 1905 wallpaper fragment of a design originally favored for use in dining rooms, hallways, and libraries. Schumacher. 7. Heart of the Wood reproduces this seventeenth-century joint stool. Such pieces were often used a small tables.

6

7

TUDOR-STYLE houses of the early twentieth century offered Americans an escape from the rigors of an ever-accelerating fast-paced life style. Houses of Old-English character were often viewed as havens where inhabitants could look beyond native roots to an English heritage that represented an assumed nobility. During an era when the United States was the final destination of millions of European immigrants, many established Americans found domestic symbols of this kind reassuring and attractive.

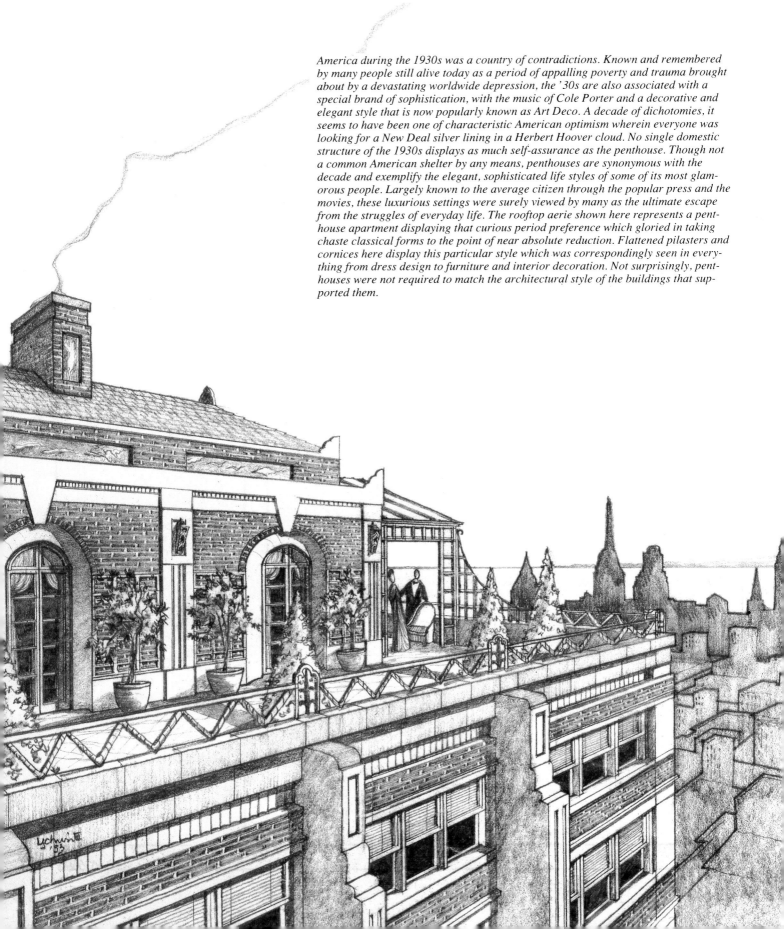

America during the 1930s was a country of contradictions. Known and remembered by many people still alive today as a period of appalling poverty and trauma brought about by a devastating worldwide depression, the '30s are also associated with a special brand of sophistication, with the music of Cole Porter and a decorative and elegant style that is now popularly known as Art Deco. A decade of dichotomies, it seems to have been one of characteristic American optimism wherein everyone was looking for a New Deal silver lining in a Herbert Hoover cloud. No single domestic structure of the 1930s displays as much self-assurance as the penthouse. Though not a common American shelter by any means, penthouses are synonymous with the decade and exemplify the elegant, sophisticated life styles of some of its most glamorous people. Largely known to the average citizen through the popular press and the movies, these luxurious settings were surely viewed by many as the ultimate escape from the struggles of everyday life. The rooftop aerie shown here represents a penthouse apartment displaying that curious period preference which gloried in taking chaste classical forms to the point of near absolute reduction. Flattened pilasters and cornices here display this particular style which was correspondingly seen in everything from dress design to furniture and interior decoration. Not surprisingly, penthouses were not required to match the architectural style of the buildings that supported them.

26
The Decade of Dichotomies (c. 1930-1940)

THE ARCHITECTURAL and interior style that is now popularly called "Art Deco" is probably best known to most Americans through the many exuberantly decorated movie palaces that appeared during the 1930s. Though undomestic in scale and even in detailing, they do epitomize some of the features that have come to be associated with interior design of the period. Among the most characteristic hallmarks of the style were an interest in a varied—even exotic—color palette, the use of new and unusual materials —especially in residential work—and the use of rich and exotic materials.

Colors have always been associated with specific periods of interior design, and those used during the 1930s are no exception. Among the most novel were the especially striking combinations of colors, including royal blues, purples, and lacquer reds; lemon yellows, lime greens, and turquoise blues; and soft grays and pearl tones. Metallic colors, including gold, copper, and silver, were often applied to papers and used on walls and ceilings. Such unusual materials as bronze and aluminum had

the advantage of being able to be cast into decorative panels and screens and found use not only in public buildings, but in fine residences as well. In contrast, walls and furniture were often made of, or covered with veneers of, such beautifully figured woods as curly maple, walnut, thuyawood, padouk, and Macassar ebony. As a further embellishment, the finest work could boast inlays of brightly colored lacquers, even rarer woods, and ivory.

The illustration above shows a penthouse salon and its adjacent gallery. Highly figured maple unifies both spaces and has even been used to fabricate some of the custom-made furniture. In the gallery, individual squares of parchment have been used to cover the walls and serve as a neutral background for a collection of art and sculpture. As a contrast, the walls of the salon are covered with a lushly patterned wallpaper of exotic tropical leaves in a color combination that includes various shades of lavender, blue green, and lime green, on a gray background.

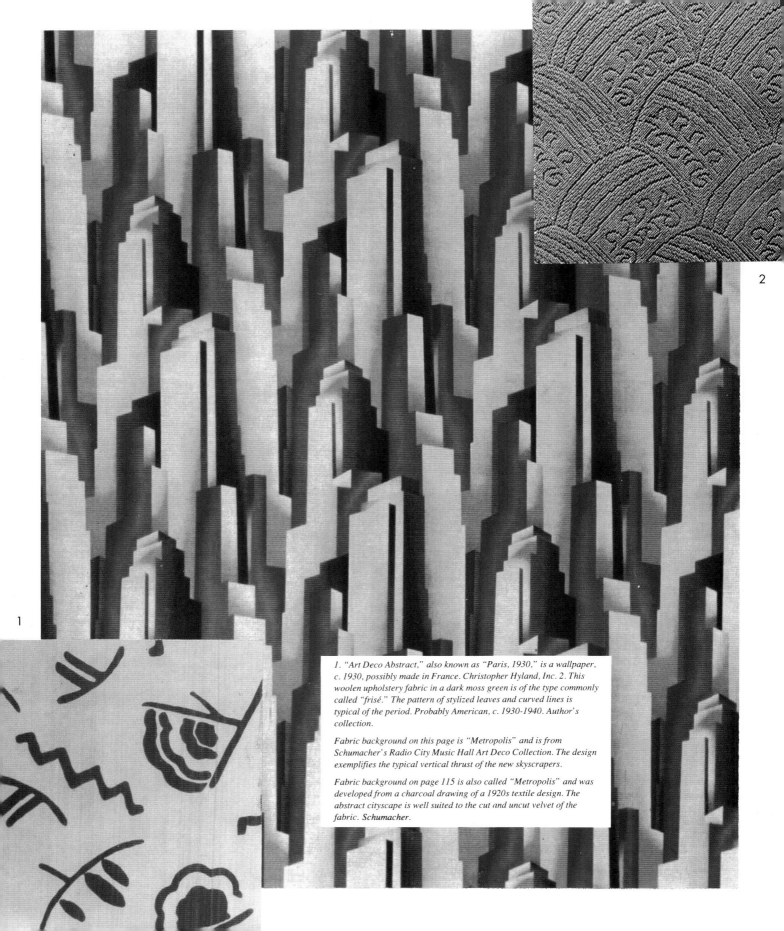

1. "Art Deco Abstract," also known as "Paris, 1930," is a wallpaper, c. 1930, possibly made in France. Christopher Hyland, Inc. 2. This woolen upholstery fabric in a dark moss green is of the type commonly called "frisé." The pattern of stylized leaves and curved lines is typical of the period. Probably American, c. 1930-1940. Author's collection.

Fabric background on this page is "Metropolis" and is from Schumacher's Radio City Music Hall Art Deco Collection. The design exemplifies the typical vertical thrust of the new skyscrapers.

Fabric background on page 115 is also called "Metropolis" and was developed from a charcoal drawing of a 1920s textile design. The abstract cityscape is well suited to the cut and uncut velvet of the fabric. Schumacher.

ALTHOUGH the Art Deco period in America lasted for only a short span of time, its influence and popularity have persisted in varying degree to the present day. Perhaps some of the style's appeal lies in its use of unusual colors and color combinations, and in forms and patterns that echo the vitality and spirit of the twentieth century. As each of the designs on these facing pages show, Art Deco design also reflects a high degree of sophistication, urban excitement, and movement.

During the 1930s an architectural style characterized by a stark simplicity, an economy of detail, an implied sense of horizontality, and an overwhelming whiteness was first seen on the American landscape. These buildings, which were invariably flat-roofed, were in sharp contrast with the traditional concepts of buildings known to most Americans, and especially with the historicist and ornamented structures with which all were familiar. Buildings in the International Style—the term used to describe these kinds of buildings—tended to favor a display of structure, material honesty and technology, as well as a dearth of ornamentation. The use of windows which sometimes turned corners with butt-edged glass, glass block, and window openings constructed directly to the ceiling line further characterize the style. In a house designed with Marcel Breuer for himself and his family in Lincoln, Massachusetts, in 1937, Walter Gropius created interior spaces that had traditional associations and forms and yet enjoyed a close association with the surrounding landscape. Gropius's house also included a screened porch and, like the house above, a second-floor deck and terraces.[1]

27

The International Style in America (c. 1936-1955)

IN 1929 Ludwig Mies van der Rohe created what was probably the most idealistic and symbolic statement concerning the essence of International-Style design. Constructed for an exposition in Spain, and consequently a temporary structure, the building designed by Mies was subsequently known as the Barcelona Pavilion and exerted an influence that has lived on long after it was dismantled. Of spare simplicity, the pavilion was actually an arrangement of spaces created by a series of marble and glass walls between a floor and a ceiling. Though never intended for habitation, nor designed as a domestic space, the structure came to influence residential interiors for several decades thereafter.

While some International-Style interiors are bare and minimal and recall the architect Le Corbusier's dictum that houses are machines in which to live, others are surprisingly habitable. Walter Gropius, one of the style's best-known masters, designed a house for himself and his family in which beautifully scaled rooms and comfortable arrangements of spaces suggest the comfort and privacy that most people desire.

In the illustration above, a subtle color palette typical of the International Style and a variety of textures play against the spare monochromatic architectural space. Soft, naturally colored linen curtains hang at one window, while wooden venetian blinds provide the possibility of privacy at another. The seating area below the corner window is almost built-in and would have been designed especially for its location. It is shown covered with a handwoven wool. Conversely, the armchair is probably covered in a soft gray wool or possibly in leather. The floor could have been paved with dark gray-colored slates on top of which might have been placed one or two flat-woven dhurries or American Indian rugs of simple graphic design.

Like much of the high-style furniture of the period, the pieces shown are of a simple classical inspiration, recalling the Biedermeier and Directoire styles as well as the twentieth-century work of Ruhlmann. A light moss-green silk velvet serves as upholstery. While a lightly colored stone floor would have been appropriate in the gallery, the flooring in the salon would likely have been a simple parquet with a custom-designed border in a darker contrasting wood, atop which would be a carefully proportioned solid-colored light-gray woolen carpet.

1

1. *Both of these fabrics, "Imperial Squares" and "Imperial Triangles II," are adaptations of textiles designed by Frank Lloyd Wright for the Imperial Hotel in Toyko between 1916 and 1922. Though conceived well before the International Style took hold in America, these designs reflect the simple, straightforward elements that complement the modern architecture of the period. Schumacher. 2. There is probably no designer associated more closely with modern American textile design of the mid-twentieth century than Vera, here represented by reductionist representations of apples, pears, grapes, and other fruits arranged on wide frames. Known as "Framed Fruit," the fabric is typical for its use of lively color, pattern, and creative elements. Interestingly, in the late 1950s, Vera and her husband, George Neumann, built a house on the Hudson designed by Marcel Breuer, one of the best-known architects of the International Style. Breuer also designed Vera's showrooms. Fabric from the Schumacher Archives.*

Not surprisingly, the most enduring architectural style in the United States has consistently been that which is simply termed "colonial." Emblematic of the national heritage, it has always represented America's ideal concept of "home." From its beginnings in the Centennial of 1876 until the first few years of the twentieth century, colonial architecture suggested a revivalist style which was, by most standards, a loose interpretation of early-American and Federal detailing applied to the typical late-Victorian dwelling house. Through the years, historical perspective and scholarship brought about the development of a more accurate colonial-era house—a style that began to appear in numbers after the First World War. As were Tudor- and Spanish-Revival houses, colonial-period houses were adapted to twentieth-century needs and, like them, combined the elements of the architectural past with the skills of both architects and artisans well-trained in the design and execution of appropriate and superbly scaled details.

28

The Second Colonial Revival (1925-1950)

AN INTEREST IN American furniture and the decorative arts, begun during the Centennial of 1876, grew in perspective in the twentieth century as collectors began to view and understand artifacts within the settings in which they were originally used. Although interest in this aspect of the Colonial Revival has been often labeled "elitist," the appeal of American antiques grew steadily throughout the first half of the century. Anyone even remotely interested in the subject was aware of the massive restoration at Colonial Williamsburg and of Henry Francis du Pont's superb collection at Winterthur. These collections, like others, became the ideals to which collectors aspired or from which they drew much of their inspiration. In their earlier days, many historic museums furnished their exhibit rooms in what we now know to have been pure twentieth-century Colonial-Revival taste. As lovely as many of these rooms were, they reflected the knowledge and collecting tastes of those who assembled them. At Winterthur, for example, room settings were often organized to highlight furniture forms from one specific area, of one particular wood, or of one cabinet maker, with colors, textiles, wallcoverings, and carpets all carefully selected to create a dazzling feast for the eyes. As such, Winterthur is in part not only a repository of superb items, but valuable for our understanding of twentieth-century collecting and taste.

Other museums—-Colonial Williamsburg and Old Sturbridge Village, for example—have continuously refurnished and reinterpreted their exhibitions as research and scholarship have clarified the details of the past. Through them, we have a clearer understanding than ever before of our historic and cultural patrimony. The elevation above represents the fireplace wall of a twentieth-century Colonial-Revival house about 1950. This is clearly the room of a collector. The most noticeable collection, and there are several, is an assemblage of nineteenth-century silhouettes. Others include pieces of French red-painted toleware and Chinese export porcelain. The sprinking of antique furniture includes a drop-leaf table, an early-nineteenth-century girandole mirror, and a Philadelphia Chippendale-style chair. Other pieces represent high-quality reproductions. Colors and fabrics reflect popular interpretations and adaptations of actual documentary artifacts. Unlike the room illustrating the first Colonial Revival (page 81), which is still essentially late-nineteenth-century in its reliance on eclectic nonrelated objects and furniture placement, the room above is more conscious in its efforts to "look colonial." Ideally, the hardwood floor in a room such as this would be covered with a fine oriental carpet, with colors complementing the walls and textiles.

1. *A mid-twentieth-century reproduction of an early-nineteenth-century covered goblet. 2. This fabric, called "Williamsburg Grapes," was the first print design reproduced by Schumacher for Colonial Williamsburg. First appearing in 1942, it reproduces an English document c. 1790. 3. "Blue Bowpot," a small dish made by Spode. 4. This silver-plated teapot was purchased as an antique and given as an anniversary gift in 1942. 5. Early-nineteenth-century needlework pictures like this one were avidly collected during the 1930s, '40s, and '50s. The frame is c. 1930. 6. The 1960 catalog of furniture reproductions available from Colonial Williamsburg notes that this table was inspired by an antique then in the Wythe House parlor. Kittinger. 7. A mid-nineteenth-century view of the White House, probably taken from a book. 8. This chair is a reproduction of a Baltimore-style fancy chair similar to one used by Lafayette during an American visit and was probably made c. 1940.*

Wallpaper background on page 123 is Schumacher's "Fox Grape," a reproduction of a French paper, c. 1780-1810, found in a building in Williamsburg.

COLONIAL-REVIVAL interiors of the 1930s, '40s, and '50s are often characterized by an eclectic assemblage of furnishings and decorative objects. The effect is often cozy and almost always charming. These were not period interiors where one decorative style predominated, but rather interiors that reflected the broad American heritage and the importance of the family home.

The present century, more than any other, has made decent and affordable housing a priority for the masses. During its first decades, the bungalow—built according to ideologies espoused by Gustav Stickley and others—fulfilled many young families' dreams of a home of their own. After the Depression and World War II, a resurgent economy enabled a whole new generation to realize similar dreams. In unprecedented numbers, ranches, Cape Cods, and split levels, like the one shown here, appeared in what had often only recently been meadows or pastures. Location often played a part in their appearance, such that, for example, the house above, with its six-over-six sash and its six-panel door reflected the colonial heritage of its Northeast setting.

29

The Baby Boomer Era (1945-1960)

IN RECENT YEARS curators and scholars have recognized that the not so distant past is, in many respects, as important in understanding the broader aspects of history as the more remote past. This philosophy is nicely illustrated at the Strawbery Banke Museum in Portsmouth, New Hampshire, where the interior of at least one late-eighteenth-century house contains two rooms decorated as they might have been about 1950, when the house was still lived in. Visitors to the Drisco House (c. 1794) will be surprised to find a living room furnished with rock maple furniture, what appears to be a Naugahyde hassock, a large cabinet-style television set, and a profusion of crocheted afghans, pillows, and doilies in a variety of gaudy colors.[1] In my recollection of the interiors of the 1950s of my childhood, there seem to have been at least three general decorating schemes in the homes of my friends and relatives. The first was what was then called "early American" and was characterized by maple armed furniture, dry sinks often used to house phonographs, and small-patterned wallpapers and fabrics. The second was generically called "modern" and usually consisted of straight-lined furniture, minimal pattern that functioned as a strong accent, and brick-faced fireplaces or planters filled with philodendrons often serving as room dividers. The third and most familiar to me was the kind of decoration my parents had in their home; my mother called it "Duncan Phyfe." Perhaps more accurately called "mahogany classical," this mid-century mode was characterized by furniture in a vaguely early-nineteenth-century English style, with saber-shaped legs, urn- or lyre-shaped forms,

and leather-topped tables and desks. The most impressive element of my family's living room was clearly the slipcovers, which were used on upholstered armchairs and on the high-armed camel-backed sofa, which is still a family favorite. Among my favorites was a set made of flowered cotton upon which rose-pink and pale-yellow roses and their green leaves stood in contrast against a black background. Plain black cotton was used on the outside arms of the furniture and for a wide border at the bottom of the very full ruffles. Completing the room were white china lamps in the shapes of urns, a floor or bridge lamp, and the all-important television set, enclosed in a mahogany cabinet with folding doors. White metal venetian blinds hung at each of the windows together with café curtains and matching valences. The walls of the room were painted a very soft, pale pastel green, and the hardwood floor was covered with a stone-green loop carpet. The room elevation above evokes childhood memories of my family's living room, though it is housed in a structure similar to the one shown on page 124. Though rooms in the pages of *House and Garden* and other shelter magazines suggest that stylish professionally decorated interiors existed in this booming postwar era, the majority inhabited by young married couples and their children were similar to those I remember. What is especially noteworthy about them is that housewives most often conceived and executed much of their own interior decoration, inspired both by that they saw in the popular magazines and by the products and materials increasingly available for their use.

1. A decorative shallow brass dish, intended for hanging on a wall, c. 1950. 2. Glazed cotton chintz originally used for draperies and bedspreads in the author's parents' home. Manufacturer unknown, c. 1943. Pastel portraits of children were popular during the 1950s. The author's sister, 1958. 4. Bunches of roses were ubiquitous decorations of the period. The wooden tray was purchased in 1950. The stone-blue background color was fashionable during the late 1940s and early '50s. 5. Women often collected English china teacups and cake plates—no two sets alike. These were generally displayed on two- or three-tiered hanging mahogany shelves. 6. A gray-on-gray wool carpet, c. 1950. 7. Magazine racks were essential for holding current issues of the widely popular weeklies and monthlies. 8. This white porcelain lamp, also shown in the photograph at left, originally had a similar silk shade with small burgundy-colored swags at its top. 9. Christmas, 1955. Note the flowered slipcovers with their black background and the tightly loomed solid-color carpet. 10. This mahogany desk chair, c. 1945, recalls designs of the early nineteenth century. It typifies the sensuous, curvilinear neoclassical styling popular with many during the period.

ARTHUR SANDERSON AND SONS is a company renowned for its elegant flowered chintzes. This one, called "Burford," is a vibrantly colored pattern of lush pink and red peonies, buds, and green leaves against a striking black background. This glazed cotton recalls fabrics of similar style and color that enjoyed great popularity in the United States during the late 1940s and early 1950s.

In 1967, Dorothy Rodgers, the wife of composer Richard Rodgers, wrote a book called The House In My Head in which she described the dream of designing and building a new country house. The book struck a chord in me and nourished my own interests in domestic building and decoration, especially in the creation of a home for myself. My inspiration, though influenced by the things around me, is, like everyone's, born of my own personality, interests, style of living and entertaining, and, most importantly, my budget. Set on the side of a hill, the house in my head is inspired by one designed by Alexander Jackson Davis and originally built for L. B. Browne at Rahway, New Jersey, around 1850. Downing describes the house in The Architecture of Country Houses (Design XXIII) as "Tuscan." [1] I have always been attracted to its general form, which reminds me of Jefferson's first version of Monticello (1770). Since I am interested in gardening, the house has been placed among a series of outside spaces or "rooms" which double the house's small size (400 square feet) and give me pleasure when both inside and outside.

30

Working It Out for Yourself

HAVING GROWN UP on a 300-year-old farm where the discovery of early artifacts was a common occurrence, I have been an inveterate collector since childhood. Today, my collection is best described as eclectic and includes furniture and objects from many periods. Though nothing is truly rare or valuable, everything has personal meaning and is linked in some way with some person or event I cherish. The perspective view on this page illustrates a "sketch problem" I undertook to formulate ideas about creating a library-studio-workroom for myself, using some of my collected treasures. Since I designed it for this book, I've included the kinds of objects and elements featured in earlier chapters. The fabrics and the color of the walls, for example, are historically accurate and appropriate for use in contemporary room settings, though not necessarily in period rooms.

Seen across an oak office table from the 1930s that I use as a desk is a fine Federal-style mantelpiece of a style associated with New York City. It is shown repainted in a bottle-green very similar to its original color. Above it hangs the wax carpet, shown on page 131, that, despite its seasonal theme, is enjoyed throughout the year. A Shaker table, a late-eighteenth-century tea table, a late-nineteenth-century Windsor chair, and a Mission-style drafting board are the principal furnishings. Decorative objects include pieces of blue-and-white Chinese, Japanese, Dutch, and English porcelain, a collection of colorful geometric-patterned oriental carpets, and a copper-based lamp made from a whiskey still my grandfather used during Prohibition. A collection of early-twentieth-century family portraits has been hung above the bookcases, but in new frames replacing the gaudy originals. Completing the nostalgic quality of the room is the old chestnut boarding salvaged from my family's old barn shortly before it was demolished for encroaching housing developments.

1. A Melas prayer carpet purchased as a travel souvenir. Turkish, c. 1900. 2., 3. A grandfather's souvenirs of service in the Kaiser's army. German, c. 1906. 4. Bits of history: the discoveries made by an immigrant family while working the fields. Artifacts include a peddler's badge (1915), shards of eighteenth- and nineteenth-century pottery and ceramics, pewter and silver buttons, and Native-American implements. 5. The timeworn sign from a family business. 6. A childhood drawing worked in needlepoint and made into a pillow. 7. This wedding photograph was colored with pastels and placed in a typical early-twentieth-century parlor frame, 1914. 8., 9. Childhood silhouettes, c. 1955. 10. A "wax carpet," intended for placement beneath a Christmas tree to catch candle drippings. American, c. 1850-1900. 11. The use of reproduction fabrics can evoke the spirit of the past in contemporary settings. This is Schumacher's "Tissu Fleuri," c. 1790, for the Colonial Williamsburg Foundation. 12. A silver nut dish, c. 1940. 13. Green handwoven cotton checked material from Textile Reproductions.

9

10

7

8

12

11

13

OLD AND FAMILIAR objects, but not necessarily rare and costly, are sometimes all that are required to give a new home a sense of the past. For many people, furnishing and living in a strictly designed period setting is impractical, if not far too expensive. Many of us, who can only appreciate the authentic from afar, can still surround ourselves with tokens of the past, items that though seldom costly are valuable reminders of many meaningful associations.

Working It Out for Yourself 131

APPENDICES

Some Notes about Period Colors

DURING THE PAST decade and a half, the determination of our colorful past has become more and more a precise science. Whereas in the past historians determined historic color evidence through a "scrape and match" process, scientists today are able to investigate and examine painted materials under the close scrutiny of sophisticated polarized-light microscopes. This process enables experts, often known as "architectural coatings specialists" or historic color analysts," to examine colors so closely they can see the various pigments that characterize each painted surface. For example, the naked eye may see a faded example of historic color on a piece of paneling or a door frame and assume that it is either the same color originally there or one that has faded over time. We now know, however, that some colors not only fade over time, but that some change because of exposure to light. One of the most common changes occurs when blues—often called "fugitive colors" in early paint history—turn into what appear to be greens. In addition, some blues—now greens—get coated with dust and dirt and then appear to unwary investigators as dull greens. No wonder that popular theory has traditionally maintained that early Americans favored a dusty, subdued color palette of grayed blues, soft greens, and dull stone colors!

Historic documentation indicates that our seventeenth-century Puritan forebears were, somewhat surprisingly, lovers of vibrant color. As noted in chapter 1, champfers on beams and posts were frequently painted in black or red, and furniture was often highlighted with touches of bright color as well. One account left to us by the diarist Samuel Sewall of Boston notes that, in 1695, a Mr. Torrey, together with his new wife, visited the Sewalls and "was much pleas'd with our painted shutters; [and] in pleasancy said he thought he had been got into paradice." These shutters were possibly interior ones, and we have no idea how they were painted. They may have been finished in a rather sophisticated trompe l'oeil technique that imitated wooden panels, much like an extant door painted a few years earlier in a nearby house eventually occupied by Paul Revere.

The colors shown here could have been found in a New England house during the last quarter of the seventeenth century. The early colonials used whitewash, sometimes—though not always—applied to interior brick walls, beams, and plaster. The color names are provided merely to distinguish the colors shown and have no intentional or specific historic reference. (Note that printed color in a book only *approximates* natural color. Printed color is made up of tiny dots of primary colors our eyes *interpret*, falsely, as true.)

a = red, *b* = blue, *c* = green, *d* = yellow, *e* = black.

Eighteenth-century Americans continued the earliest settlers' love for bold, bright colors within their interiors and often painted the prominent paneled fireplace walls of their houses in especially striking color combinations. Early restorations have often erroneously led us to believe that these Americans favored rather dull and dusty tones, with the result that many of the colors now associated with the twentieth-century colonial revival echo these kinds of colors. More recent research, however, has suggested quite the opposite—the uncovering of a surprisingly brilliant color palette, consisting not only of the expected dark reds, stones, and grays, but also of vivid greens, bright blues, and even startling yellows and pumpkin-toned hues. At Gunston Hall, the restored eighteenth-century mansion of patriot George Mason, the walls of the central hallway have been recently repainted with a striking bright blue. A similar color was enjoyed by his neighbors, the Washingtons, who painted the paneled walls of their parlor in this fashionable and expensive color. Today's Mount Vernon features this color and one that is perhaps even more memorable. In the Washingtons' drawing room, the walls and elaborate rococo fireplace surround have been repainted the same bright green that the general would have remembered at the end of the century.

The colors shown here represent a variety of those used in many American houses during the second half of the eighteenth century.

During the nineteenth century, color preferences in America mirrored the widening availability of an increasingly varied color palette. One book, *Directions for House and Ship Painting* (1812) by Hezekiah Reynolds, specifically notes interior colors and offers directions for their preparation. The book is a fascinating roster of early-nineteenth-century colors. Included are "recipes" for colors called "Ice, Light Stone, Sea Green, Prussian Blue, Navy Blue, Dark Stone, Red, Purple, Claret, and Chocolate." Reynolds also provides directions for making mahogany, red cedar, and "cherrytree wood," used for graining, and for marble color. Other popular colors during this period—especially in high-style interiors— were those inspired by the archaeological discoveries at Pompeii. These included rich earth-colored reds, sky blues, sunny yellows, mineral greens, and black. The colors shown here suggest these fashionable tones.

a = dark gray, b = medium gray, c = blue, d = rose, e = dusty green, f = gold, g = dark brown or walnut, h = pumpkin, i = bright green, j = sky blue.

i

a = pearl, b = medium stone, c = sea green,
d = Pompeiian brown, e = sunflower, f = bright blue,
g = dark mineral green, h = light olive, i = black.

By mid-century, Americans were becoming increasingly interested in a color palette that included deep, bright blues, maroons, rose, bold greens, crimsons, and gold. Developments in industrial technology were making brighter colors a reality as artificial pigments began to replace natural ones. The colors shown here are typical of the kinds that appeared in wallpapers, carpets, and textiles of the period.

By the last quarter of the nineteenth century, interior decoration had become a very careful orchestration wherein the colors of walls, ceilings, floors, furnishings, textiles, and decorative objects worked as a harmonious whole. Color preferences had changed again, in large measure because of the increasing availability of ready-mixed paints and more varied and sophisticated pigments. Strong ideas and theories about color appeared, and strict concepts were set down for the painting and decorating of all interior surfaces. Most theorists specified the acceptability of specific colors for specific rooms. Drawing rooms, for example, which were the general preserve of those of a "delicate character," were ideally suited to colors such as pale apricot, pale blue, and lemon yellow. Libraries, on the other hand, were thought to be most appropriate when furnished in deep, rich, and somber tones.

Among the wide range of colors found in the late-Victorian house are the following:

a = bright blue, b = dark maroon, c = rose, d = bold green,
e = purple, f = gold, g = bold blue, h = dark crimson.

i

a = *light olive, b* = *medium olive, c* = *dark olive, d* = *claret,*
e = *golden brown, f* = *bright blue (accent),*
g = *vestibule terra cotta, h* = *old gold, i* = *ashes of roses.*

The most characteristic colors in the American home during the first two decades of the twentieth century were those which echoed the natural hues advocated by Gustav Stickley. In his writings, and most notably in *The Craftsman*, Stickley mentions the character of natural materials and glories in the processes he had developed for achieving the best finishes for his furniture. Within Craftsman-style interiors, the essential colors were derived from the coppers used on hearth hoods and lamp bases, from the natural and light-toned green of wicker chairs and settees, from the natural linens embroidered with designs of ginkgo leaves and pine cones, from the muted tones of handmade pottery, and from the soft glow of the oak and chestnut furniture and paneling.

a = *olive green, b* = *late autumn gold, c* = *dark brown,*
d = *stony teal, e* = *russet.*

Tips on Undertaking an Interior Design Project

Planning Your Project

MOST HOME decorating projects fall short of initial intentions because of poor planning. This is as true for projects involving one room as for a number of rooms. In the latter situation, of course, the results can be especially disastrous.

Whether or not you're using professional assistance or are doing most of the work yourself, you will find that a clearly delineated list of goals and objectives—an understanding of just what it is you want to achieve—is essential for success. If you are working with architects, interior designers, or other professional specialists, they will appreciate both your understanding of the project and the ability to furnish them with as much information as you can. Good design and the best results come from good working relationships, and you will find that the carefully selected professionals you work with are there to assist you towards making your ideas a reality.

To begin, here are some important questions to ask yourself before getting down to the serious business of interior design:

- What do I want to accomplish? Are my goals realistic?
- Can I really create an *authentic* architectural period interior, or should I, instead, use fabrics, wallcovering, and colors to *suggest* a historical setting?
- Can I afford to do what I'd like to, or should I take a closer look at costs?
- Can I plan my project in phases so that I may better complete this as my budget allows? If I do this, what needs to be done first, and in what sequence should the remainder be done?
- How long will the work take to complete? Can I realistically live in a partially completed environment for a number of months, or even years?
- Should I be thinking about professional assistance? Perhaps I can get some valuable information about planning the entire project?
- Where do I find craftspeople and suppliers with the background and feeling for this kind of specialized project?
- Does my project require architectural and structural work? Will permits be required, or the services of a structural engineer, plumber, or other professional?

- Do I know enough about what I want to do? Do I really have a clear understanding of the historic style I wish to replicate?
- Should I read and study more, or even take a few courses?
- Do I know where to find the answers to these and the many other questions bound to arise before my project is completed?

Of course there comes a point when you just have to begin. Be certain to set firm goals, think about options, and know who to ask when the inevitable questions come up along the way. Never be afraid that what you have to ask may sound foolish. Remember the old adage that "the more you know, the more you know you need to know." After all, even the experts are learning every day.

Taking Measurements and Preparing Drawings

Supplies Needed

- A pad of plain grid paper at least 8½" x 11" and a clipboard.
- A 50-foot tape measure.
- A six-foot carpenter's ruler.
- Several sharpened No. 2 pencils with erasers and a pencil sharpener.
- Several sharpened red pencils.
- An instant camera *and* a 35mm. camera (for documentation).
- A flashlight.
- Enough time and patience to measure carefully.

If you are seriously thinking about getting involved in your own project, you will need to learn as much as you can about the space you plan to renovate. The best way is to measure the space and draw it as a floor plan. With a bit of practice and by following the simple procedures that follow, you should be able to create a basic architectural drawing that will prove essential as you begin to design your project. Remember, you do not need to produce an exhibit-quality drawing. Here are some suggestions:

- Find a partner who will be able to help you. It is very difficult to handle a measuring tape by yourself.

- When you gain entry to the space, draw a simple freehand floor plan as close to scale as you can on a sheet of paper. Make sure to leave room to record dimensions and notes. Use a lead pencil to draw the plan elements.

- Indicate all architectural features such as windows, doors, fireplaces, and door-swings on this freehand plan.

- Determine the compass points and include an arrow facing north somewhere at the base of the drawing. This will be helpful later when considering window treatments and the need to control glare and light.

- Be sure to include wall thickness dimensions in areas where an opening leads—for example, into an alcove or hallway.

- Measure and record all door and window frames, baseboards, ceiling and cornice moldings, chair rails, and any other decorative features which will effect the interior. You may find the use of a molding profile, available in most hardware stores, of particular help.

- Note the location of light switches, electrical outlets, lighting fixtures, plumbing features, radiators, appliances, and any other things that will either remain or need to be removed. If a gas stove, for example, must be removed, you will need to call the proper authorities. *Never* attempt to do any electrical, plumbing, or gas-line work yourself.

- Note the location of electrical boxes, if there are any in the room. Like plumbing, these are costly to remove and your re-decoration scheme may have to address camouflaging them while maintaining accessibility.

- Note the height of the room—that is, the distance from the finished floor to the finished ceiling. Circle this direction and place it somewhere on the sheet, making sure to label it.

- If there are beams or other special ceiling features such as skylights, you may want to consider drawing a ceiling plan and a section through the space.

- Now take overall dimensions of each side of the room. When you have completed this, take diagonal measurements from corner to corner. These will serve as checks later on and let you know if the room is out of square. Use a red pencil to record all dimensions.

- Finally, you are ready to begin measuring in a logical progresion around the room. It is best to proceed in a clockwise direction. Measure only to the nearest half inch. You only need to record more exacting measurements when you are drawing details. One person should be responsible for calling off the measurements while the other does the recording.

- When you have completed this task, take instant photographs of overall views and of specific details that will assist you to hard-line your drawing after you've left the space (assuming, of course, that the space is not yet yours by sale or lease).

- Don't be surprised if you have to return to the space afterwards to clarify dimensions or record something that you've forgotten. If you own, or live in, the space, this will not be a problem, but if you need to make arrangements with the present owner, you may want to be especially careful to make certain that you get all necessary information the first time around.

- Of course, before you do anything else, make sure to identify the drawing and record the date, as well.

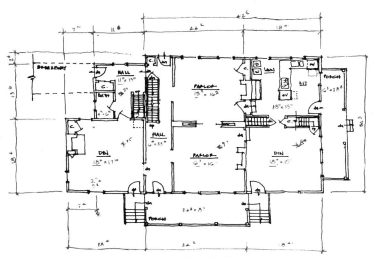

Herbert J. Githens, Architect, Montclair, New Jersey

Hard-Lining Drawings from Field Observations

Preparing an accurate architectural drawing from your field drawings and notes is called "hard-lining," because what you are actually doing is taking your freehand plan and translating it into an accurately drawn architectural plan. This will probably take a little practice but by studying completed floor-plan drawings, you should be able to get the idea rather quickly. Remember, these drawings are only intended for your use and are a tool to assist you as you plan your project. Any architect or designer you may hire will likely prepare his own, although your field drawings and observations will likely be very useful to him.

Supplies Needed

- A good flat drawing surface. You can purchase one with parallel rules already attached. (T-squares are obsolete.) An 18" x 24" board is a good size for home use.

- A variety of triangles (a 30°/60° and a 45°), or one good adjustable triangle.

- A circle template.

- An architect's scale with $1/8$", $1/4$", $3/8$", and $3/4$" scales.

- Lead holders and leads such as 2H, 4H, and H, and a sharpener for mechanical pencils.

- A good soft white eraser.

  Drafting tape.

- A good-quality drafting vellum capable of blueline reproduction. This can be purchased in pads, and is less costly than buying a roll.

- A roll of yellow tracing paper. The smallest roll is easiest to handle.

How to Get Started

- Choose a convenient scale such as $1/4$" = 1'-0". If the room you are drawing is quite small, you may want to choose a scale such as $1/2$" = 1'-0" or whatever you feel will produce a drawing large enough to work with. Do not forget to note the scale chosen on the drawing.

- With the scale determined, decide where to locate your drawing on the sheet, taking care to leave room for notes.

- You are now ready to transfer your field measurements onto the vellum. You should do this in the same order in which they were recorded.

- Make sure you draw firmly, so that the lines will be dark enough to reproduce during the printing process. You can lay out the dimensions by drawing lightly with a 2H pencil and then going over these "construction lines" in a heavier hand with the same pencil lead when you are certain about the dimensions. It may be necessary during this phase to re-check some of your measurements.

- Use the accepted conventions for noting electrical outlets, door-swings, and other architectural information. See sample floor plans for examples.

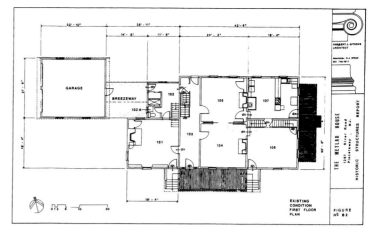

Herbert J. Githens, Architect, Montclair, New Jersey

- You may decide not to put dimensions or notes on the finished plan, but rather use it solely as a background for your design schemes. Dimensions can be recorded on another print for references and documentation.

A Note about Drawing Elevations

As applied to interior design, elevations are drawings of the walls of rooms and can be drawn at any convenient scale. (For clarity, you may wish to draw them at the same scale as the floor plans, or choose a slightly smaller scale such as $3/8$".) When you are recording information at the site, you will want to draw simple elevations of each wall and note all pertinent architectural information on them. Such information will include the size, location, and dimension of windows and doors, scaled measurements of their design, the dimensions of baseboards, cornices, and other features as well as the location of any electrical, plumbing, and heating elements. In short, record and draw elevations in the same way you would a room's floor plans. Many of the drawings in the thirty main chapters of this book are elevations, though they have gone beyond the general understanding of a purely architectural elevation.

Creating a Simple Perspective Sketch

One especially useful tool used by professional designers is the thumbnail perspective sketch. This is a quick three-dimensional view often created during design meetings with clients to demonstrate a concept about the space being designed. Such sketches can easily be made into more finished perspectives with more time and effort. With a basic understanding of what a perspective drawing is and a little practice, you, too, can easily master the technique. Here are some hints:

- Think of all lines in a room as vanishing to one ultimate point. This is called the vanishing point. The perspective view on page 73, for example, demonstrates this principle. Can you find the vanishing point?

- Take a piece of paper and draw the far wall of a hypothetical room. Now place a vanishing point somewhere within that elevation (see drawing 'a').

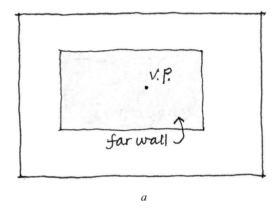

a

- The next step is to provide the far wall with adjacent walls, a floor, and a ceiling—in other words, to create the illusion of an enclosed space (or room) by extending lines drawn from the vanishing point to each of the four corners of the room's far wall (see drawing 'b').

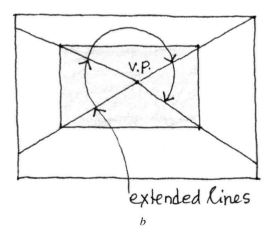

b

- Now erase the lines you drew within the far wall elevation (see drawing 'c').

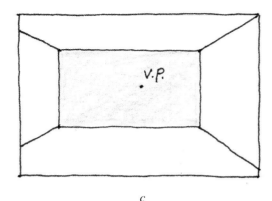

c

- Using the same vanishing point and the same idea of extended lines, draw in a door and a window wherever you wish. For example, to determine the height and proportions of a window on a side wall, draw extended lines to points on the vertical edge of the far wall which represent the sill and head of the window. Extend these lines to the side wall. Now draw two vertical lines to "fix" the sides of the window opening. Of course, you will have to "guesstimate" proportions. In a measured perspective, you would be able to accurately plot dimensions (see drawing 'd'). Again, *all* lines will vanish to the vanishing point.

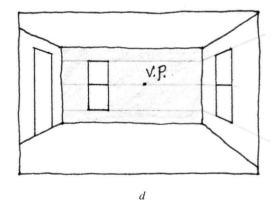

d

- After practicing this for a while, you will note that a view into a room can be changed by altering the position of the vanishing point. If you want to make it seem as if you are looking up to the ceiling, for example, place the vanishing point near the floor line of the rear wall (see drawing 'e').

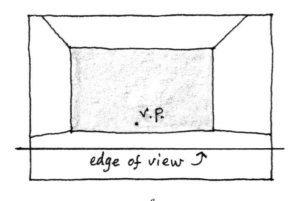

e

- To position furniture and other decorative objects within the space, use the same basic principles noted above, but locate these items *on the floor* rather than on the walls, and extend all lines to the vanishing point as earlier. By practicing and becoming familiar with the procedure, you should eventually be able to place furniture on angles. Of course, in a quick technique such as this, you will have to fill in many of the details with freehand drawing (see drawing 'f').

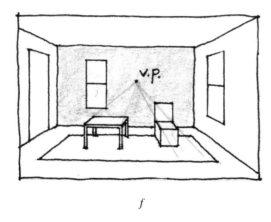

f

If you wish to learn more about the real technique of perspective drawing, consult one of the many books written on the subject. Of course, many design offices now generate perspective sketches by computer, though nothing will ever replace one's ability to draw these quick sketches oneself.

Finding Expert Help

Most projects necessitate a degree of expertise requiring professional assistance. For example, if you need to remove or add walls, relocate or remove plumbing, install heating, or restore a damaged plaster ceiling, you will need to rely upon the services of specialists. In most jurisdictions, laws dictate that such work as structural changes, plumbing installation, and electrical alterations needs to be done under the supervision of a licensed architect.

Many of the textiles and wallpapers most appropriate for your project may also have to be purchased through an architect or interior designer. Designing historically accurate interiors is generally not as easy as one might expect. Most decorative elements are not available at the local home center, and some may even have to be produced especially for your project. Do not be disheartened by this. Help is available, and there are many architects, interior designers, architectural historians, and other specialists well able to guide and assist you over the hurdles. Many will be willing to help you with specific parts of your project, so you need not fear that they will necessarily have to be retained for every phase. Talk with them and you will find most more than willing to help you along.

Finding architects sympathetic to historic interiors can begin with a telephone call to the local chapter of the American Institute of Architects. You can also contact your state's preservation office, usually located in the state capital, for a list of architects recognized as able to undertake historic work. Naturally, you should also speak with people you know who have had such work done in the past. Visit specific sites and talk with both architects and clients before making any decisions. Local historical societies are also good places to inquire about competent restoration architects.

Interior designers with specific expertise in historic interiors can be found in much the same manner, although you will want to contact the American Society of Interior Designers. Many restoration architects will also be familiar with professionals working in this field, and many have a regular working relationship with historic interiors specialists and other professionals.

Finding a carpenter capable of working in a restoration setting is a slightly more difficult matter. The best are often booked well into the future and work almost exclusively with specific architects. The best advice on finding a capable carpenter and other craftspeople is to inquire of architects and designers you may have contacted or, again, with local historical societies. State preservation offices also frequently maintain lists of craftspeople capable of working in this field.

You may not find the experts you need overnight, but with some perseverance and a little creative sleuthing, you will be able to locate all the help you need. Just be aware that not everyone who professes to be proficient is necessarily able to produce the quality of work which historic design demands. Be discriminating and well prepared to ask prospective architects and designers the best questions concerning their abilities to undertake your project.

How and Where to Learn More

One thing is certain—the more involved you become in your project, the more you'll learn and the more interested you'll become in learning more. Household renovation and restoration projects of any kind have a way of dominating one's life—especially during the process—-and you will be surprised at how much you will learn as you go along.

Here are some things you can do to learn to improve your knowledge of historic styles, historic buildings, the decorative arts, and the process of design:

- Read as much as you can. Start by perusing the bibliography at the end of this book.

- Diversify your reading within the subject so that you are not learning about just one aspect of it. For example, if you are interested in seventeenth-century America, read various histories and diaries, books about period furniture and the decorative arts, and visit a number of historic sites where you can see both original structures and places where period living conditions have been re-created.

- Join such organizations that produce periodicals and disseminate information as the National Trust for Historic Preservation, the Association of Preservation Technology, and state or local historical societies.

- Visit museums where you can see historic interiors that have been accurately preserved and re-created. These include such places as Colonial Williamsburg, Old Sturbridge Village, those administered by the Society for the Preservation of New England Antiquities, and others of like stature.

- Enroll in courses or attend lectures and conferences dealing with a variety of preservation and historic architectural issues.

- Subscribe to magazines and periodicals featuring historic interiors. Not only are the photographs frequently evocative, but many cover buildings and sites that are relatively unknown. Of particular value are advertisements for professional services that often appear at the back of these periodicals. In this regard, *The Old House Journal* (435 Ninth Street, Brooklyn NY 11215) is especially valuable.

- Visit antique shops, an immensely educational and enjoyable diversion.

In short, the old cliché rings true—the best way to learn is to keep your eyes and ears open.

Sources and Information

THE FIRMS listed below are among those which can supply you with a variety of reproduction fabrics, wallpapers, carpets, and other items appropriate for use in historic interiors. While orders may be placed directly with some firms, others, as indicated, require that orders be referred through interior designers or architects.

Bradbury and Bradbury Art Wallpapers
P.O. Box 155
Benicia, CA 94510
(707) 746-1900

Catalog available.

- **Aesthetic Movement Ceiling**, from the Aesthetic Movement Roomset.
- **Bower**, English, c. 1910. Code: BOW.
- **Chequerboard Ceiling Paper**, from the Morris Tradition Roomset .
- **Claire's Willow**, English, c. 1870-1880. Code: EMF.
- **Emelita's Frieze**, American, c. 1840-1850. Code: EMF.
- **Fleur De Lys**, English, c. 1840-1850. Adaptation of larger design by Pugin. Code: FLW.
- **Honeysuckle**, English, c. 1900-1920. Code: HSW.
- **Lion and Dove Frieze**, English, c. 1900. Designed by Walter Crane, document at Victoria and Albert Museum. Special order.
- **Thistle**, English, c. 1900-1920. Code: THW.

Brunschwig & Fils, Inc.
979 Third Avenue
New York, NY 10022
(212) 838-7878

Order through designers and architects.

- **Nemours Cotton and Linen Print**, Indian, c. 1725-1775. Document at Winterthur originally hand-painted. # 78500.04.

J. R. Burrows & Co., Historical-Design Merchants
P.O. Box 522
Rockland, MA 02370
(617) 982-1812 (tel), (617) 982-1636 (fax)

Brochure available.

J. R. Burrows & Co. is the American agent for Wilton and Brussels carpets made by Woodward Grosvenor & Co., Ltd. All carpets illustrated in this book are from the archives of Woodward Grosvenor & Co., Ltd., Kidderminster, England, and are used with permission. Woodward Grosvenor carpets are copyrighted designs.

- **Aesthetic Medallion Border** (body available), c. 1889. # 8914/13.
- **Anthemion Design**, on point paper by I. Arbuthnot, c. 1805. # M398.
- **Carnation Border**, # 7624/18, and body (# 7624/10), c. 1876.
- **Chrysanthemum**, c. 1890. # 9026/10.
- **Floral Medallion**, c. 1855. Reproduction installed at Fallon House, San Jose, CA, and Tallman House, Janesville, WI. # 5550/10.
- **Green Rococo Scroll**, 1876. Reproduction installed at Capt. Forbes House, Milton, MA. # 7632/10.
- **Mildenhall**, c. 1900. # 9925/10.
- **Neo-Classic Scroll Border** (body available), 1839, #3945/17.
- **Pembroke Leaf Body** (border available), c. 1800. #0150/10.
- **Pompeiian Figures**, body and border, designed in 1806 by I. Arbuthnot. Order by name.
- **Reform Medallion Body** (border available). Reproduction installed at William H. Taft NHS, Cincinnati, OH. Order by name.
- **Rococo Medallion**, 1854. Reproduction installed at Ham House, Dubuque, IA. # 5418/10.
- **Tropical Leaves**, c. 1875. Reproduction installed at Iolani Palace, Honolulu, HI. 7545/10.
- **Tulip and Lily Runner**, designed by William Morris in 1875, produced until 1925. Worsted Wilton. # 7500/10
- **Turkey**, body and border, 1876. Order by name.
- **Turkey Medallion with Gothic Diaper Ground**, 1829. # 2964/10

Classic Revivals, Inc.
1 Design Center Place, Suite 545
Boston, MA 02210
Attn: John Buscemi
(617) 574-9030 (tel), (617) 574-9027 (fax)

- **Godolphin Damask**, European, early eighteenth century, 100% wool. Guy Evans Collection.

- **La Danse Egyptienne**, Alsace, 1827, designed by Georges Zipelius for copperplate engraving, 100% cotton. Guy Evans Collection.

- **Palmerston Damask**, English, c. 1840, a silk and wool copy of a curtain. Guy Evans Collection.

- **Oxborough Trellis**, English, c. 1870-1880, block print wallpaper of a document from Oxburgh Hall, Norfolk. The Silvergate Collection.

- **Somerton Damask**, English, c. 1680. The design probably dates from c. 1630-1640 and is from a document at Ham House. Handwoven silk. Humphries Weaving Company.

- **Walpole Damask**, European, c. 1740, 100% wool. Scale changed from document. Also available as a block print wallpaper. Guy Evans Collection

- **Willement Damask**, English, c. 1840s, 100% wool. Designed by Thomas Willement and also available in a block print wallpaper. Guy Evans Collection.

Eaton Hill Textile Works
R.D. 1, Box 970
Plainfield, VT 05667
(802) 426-3733

Makers of handwoven Venetian carpets.

Heart of the Wood
P.O. Box 3031
Plymouth, MA 02361
Attn: Ted Curtin
(508) 888-3552

- **Back Stool**, reproduction of original c. 1680 New York chair with leather upholstery, oak.

- **Joined Rocking Cradle**, reproduction of a c. 1620 English original, oak.

- **Joint Stool**, reproduction of a c. 1650 American original from Boston's North Shore, oak.

Christopher Hyland, Inc., NYC
979 Third Avenue
New York, NY 10022
(212) 688-6121

Order through designers and architects.

- **Arlesford**, English, c. 1690-1700, block print. # AB129/6.

- **Fiore**, English, c. 1750-1760, block print. # AB252.

- **Art Deco Abstract**, probably French, 1930, block print. # AB157/1.

Carol Mead
R.R. 3, Box 3396
West Addison, VT 05491
(802) 759-2692

- **Eucalpytus**

- **Riversize** (frieze)

- **Wildrose** (frieze)

Mt. Diablo Handprints
940 Tyler Street, Bldg. 56
P.O. Box 726
Benicia, CA 94510
(707) 745-3388

- **Anglo-Japanese Blossom**, American, c. 1880-1890. Machine print from an original paper in the Cohen House, Oakland, CA. # AJB-001

- **Basket Weave/Wren's Nest Hall**, American, early twentieth century. Reproduction of original at Wren's Nest, Joel Chandler Harris Association, Atlanta, GA.

- **Billings Acanthus**, American, c. 1890-1900. Machine print. Reproduction of original at Billings Farm and Museum, Woodstock, VT. # BAW-001.

- **Diamond Stripe Border**, French or American, c. 1860-1870. Reproduced for Henry Ford Museum and Greenfield Village, Dearborn, MI.

- **Henry Ford Panel Stripe**, American, c. 1860-1870. Block or machine print. Reproduced for Henry Ford Museum and Greenfield Village, Dearborn, MI.

- **Frost Grape Wall**, American, 1850s. Machine print. Reproduction of original at Stonewall Jackson's Head-quarters, Winchester, VA.

- **Hummingbird and Lattice**, French, c. 1900-1910. Block print. Reproduction of original at Kearny Mansion, Fresno, CA. # HBW-001.

- **Lincoln's Bedroom**, French, c. 1850-1860. Block print. Reproduction of original at Lincoln Home NHS, Springfield, IL. Original paper extant at Haley's Antiques, Athol, MA.

- **McFadden-Ward Floral**, American, c. 1890-1900. Reproduced from original at McFadden-Ward House, Beaumont, TX. # MFW-001.

- **Passion Flower**, French, c. 1900-1910. Block print. Reproduced from original paper at Kearny Mansion, Fresno, CA . # PFW⁻001.

- **William Taft Frieze**, American, c. 1840-1370. Machine print. Reproduction of original at William H. Taft NHS, Cincinnati, OH.

- **Wren's Nest Study**, American, 1897. Machine print. Reproduction of original at Wren's Nest, Joel Chandler Harris Association. Atlanta, GA.

Old World Weavers
A Division of Stark Carpet Corp.
979 Third Avenue
New York, NY 10022
(212) 355-7186

Order through designers and architects.

- **Horsehair, Black,** # SK06080001.

PY-WE-ACK Studio
P.O. Box 292
Monrovia, CA 91017
Attn: Ed Pinson, Debra Ware
(818) 359-6113

Catalog available.

Wallcoverings and borders hand-painted on canvas:

- **Oakhurst Border**
- **Poppy Border**
- **Sequoia Bough Border**
- **Arroyo Ginkgo Border**
- **Liberty Rose Border**

Arthur Sanderson and Sons
979 Third Avenue
New York, NY 10022
(212) 319-7220

Order through designers and architects.

- **Buford Cotton Chintz**, English, from the Eaton Chintz Collection. Glazed. # PR 7558-2.

- **Willow Bough Minor**, English machine print adaptation of William Morris's "Willow Bough," c. 1887. # WM 7676.

Scalmandré
950 Third Avenue
New York, NY 10022
(212) 980-3888

Order through designers and architects.

Fabrics:

- **America Representing at the Altar of Liberty**, English, c. 1790-1800. Printed union cloth, linen and cotton. # 11057-001.

- **Country Plaid**, cotton and linen, # 99473.

- **Andrew Jackson Floral**, French, c. 1800, 100% cotton. Block print. # 6046-1.

- **Andrew Johnson Suite**, c. 1850-1875, cotton and silk liséré repp. # 20123-001.

- **L' Escarpolette Printed Toile**, 100% cotton. # 16006 -003.

- **Pillar Printed Chintz**, English, c. 1815-1830, roller print, 100% cotton, glazed. # 7711-1.

Wallpaper:

- **Rosecliff Tuft**, French, 1856, handprint. # 81461. Also available in matching fabric. # 16065.

F. Schumacher and Co.
939 Third Avenue
New York, NY 10022
(212) 415-3900

Order through designers, architects, and select retail stores. Note, however, that Schumacher's Colonial Williamsburg Collection is also available directly from The Colonial Williamsburg Foundation. Contact Customer Service, (804) 220-7378 (catalog available).

Fabrics:

- **Bali**, a reproduction of a handprinted nineteenth-century batik from Java. From the Heritage Collection, c. 1970. Example shown from author's collection. # 66532. Special order.

- **Carolina Toile**, English, c. 1775 copperplate print. 100% cotton. Colonial Williamsburg Collection # 78830. Available in matching wallpaper, # 40-0626-3.

- **Chrysanthemum and Fern**, English, c. 1940-1970 block print. 100% cotton, glazed. # 162770.

- **Ferndale**, English (?), c. 1850. Reproduction of woolen document in wool, rayon, and cotton. From the Victorian Collection and endorsed by the Victorian

Society in America. # 73370.

- **Floral Damask**, from the Colonial Williamsburg Collection. Cotton and spun rayon. # 57112.

- **Framed Fruit**, American, c. 1950 design by Vera. Nylon press cloth. Example pictured is from the Schumacher Archives. # FS171889. Special order.

- **Gloucester Damask**, European, c. 1680-1700. Cotton and linen. Example pictured is from the Schumacher Archives. Reproduction in the Colonial Williamsburg Collection. # 52840.

- **Gobelin's Forest**. This fabric is copied from a document American wallpaper, c. 1900-1910. Cotton and linen print. Matching wallpaper available.

- **Imperial Triangles II** and **Imperial Squares**. Both of these textiles are adaptations of fabrics designed by Frank Lloyd Wright. The former is cotton and rayon; the latter is wool, cotton, acrylic, and rayon.

- **Kew Gardens Glazed Chintz**, c. 1850. Coordinating wallpaper also available.

- **Metropolis**, a fabric of cut and uncut velvet derived from a charcoal drawing of a 1920s textile design. Viscose and cotton.

- **Ogden's Floral Printed Cotton** is a fabric copied as a companion to a document American wallpaper, c. 1890-1900, in the Schumacher Archives. Fabric and wallpaper are available in floral and striped versions. Cotton sateen.

- **Tapestry for Upholstery**, c. 1910-1915. Example pictured is from the Schumacher Archives. # FS 18581. Special order.

- **Tissu Fleuri**, French, c. 1790. A Colonial Williamsburg reproduction from a wood-block print. Linen and cotton. # 161400.

- **Williamsburg Grapes** was the first printed fabric reproduced by Schumacher for Colonial Williamsburg. First introduced in 1942. Example shown is from author's collection. Special order.

- **Williamsburg Wool Moreen**, England, eighteenth century. Cotton and wool. Colonial Williamsburg Collection. # 90344.

- **Worthington**, a 100% glazed cotton screen print inspired by eighteenth-century silk brocades of LaSalle. # 162130.

Wallpaper:

- **Bernardston**, reproduction of c. 1790-1810 document in Capt. Hale House, Bernardston, MA. Colonial Williamsburg Collection.

- **Classical Urn**, French, c. 1790-1810. Colonial Williamsburg Collection.

- **Egg and Dart Border**, inspired by an architectural molding at Williamsburg's Governor's Palace. Colonial Williamsburg Collection.

- **Fox Grape**, French, c. 1780-1810. Document was found in a building in Williamsburg and is also known to have been used by Jefferson at Monticello. Matching fabric available. Colonial Williamsburg Collection.

- **Pillar and Arch**, English, c. 1760-1785. Colonial Williamsburg Collection.

Michael Stiles and Toad Hall
Murals, Paintings, and Illustrations
Studio: Box 364, Cherry Valley, NY 13320
(607) 264-3302

Toad Hall: 888 Broadway, 4th floor, New York, NY
(212) 473-3000 ext. 281

Michael Stiles is able to replicate the style and subject matter that characterizes the work of such early-American muralists as Rufus Porter.

Textile Reproductions
Box 48
West Chesterfield, MA 01084
Attn: Kathleen B. Smith
(413) 296-4437

Catalog available.

Handwoven worsted fringes; tapes of wool, linen, cotton, and silk; handwoven cotton checks (#225); handwoven small checks and stripes (# 228); linsey woolsey; wool blanketing; and colored woolens.

Thistle Hill Weavers
R.D. 2, Box 75
Cherry Valley, NY 13320
Attn: Rabbit Goody
(518) 284-2729 (tel and fax)

Weavers of machine-made Venetian carpets and coverlets.

Woodward Grosvenor & Co., Ltd.
Stourvale Mills, Green Street
Kidderminster DY10 1AT
United Kingdom
(0562) 861994

See **J. R. Burrows & Co.**

Notes

Introduction, pp. 9-11

1. Marshall B. Davidson, ed., *The American Heritage History of Colonial Antiques* (New York: American Heritage Publishing Co., 1971), p. 9.

2. Ibid.

3. Ibid., p. 67.

4. Ibid., p. 66.

5. Antoinette F. Downing and Vincent J. Scully, Jr., *The Architectural Heritage of Newport, Rhode Island 1640-1915* (New York: Bramhall House, 1967), p. 40.

6. Ibid.

7. Davidson, p. 155.

8. Carl Van Doren, *Benjamin Franklin* (New York: The Viking Press, 1938), pp. 276-277.

9. William Howard Adams, *Jefferson's Monticello* (New York: Abbeville Press, 1983), p. 220.

10. William Seale, *The President's House, A History* (Washington, D.C.: White House Historical Association, 1986), pp. 540-541.

11. Pauline C. Metcalf, ed., *Ogden Codman and the Decoration of Houses* (Boston: The Boston Athenaeum/David R. Godine, 1988), p. 9.

12. Andrew Jackson Downing, *The Architecture of Country Houses* (New York: Dover Publications, 1969), p. 18.

13. Algernon Charles Swinburne, "An Ode to England," II, 5.

1. The Earliest Colonials, pp. 12-15

1. Davidson, p. 19.

2. Abbott Lowell Cummings, *The Framed Houses of Massachusetts Bay 1625-1725* (Cambridge: Harvard University Press, 1979), pp. 192-195.

3. Ibid., p. 194.

3. The Georgians, pp. 20-23

1. William A. Flynt and Joseph Peter Spang, "Exterior Architectural Embellishment," *The Magazine Antiques* (March, 1985), 633.

4. Fashionable, Plain, and Neat, pp. 24-27

1. Hunter Dickinson Farish, ed., *Journals and Letters of Philip Vickers Fithian 1773-1774* (Virginia: Colonial Williamsburg, 1965), pp. 80-81.

2. Ibid., p . 95.

3. Ibid., p . 81.

4. Many of these "personal shoppers" chose items reflecting their own tastes, much to the annoyance of their colonial clients.

5. In a letter to his English factor, an exasperated Washington wrote : "It is needless for me to particularize the sorts, quality, or taste I woud choose to have them in unless it is observd, and you may believe me when I tell you that instead of getting things good and fashionable in their several kinds we often have articles sent us that could only have been usd by our Forefathers in the days of yore. . . ."

6. Graham Hood, "Early Neoclassicism in America, " *The Magazine Antiques* (December, 1991), 981.

7. Sideboards in the form which we associate them first appeared in the late eighteenth century.

8. A superb example from a parlor at "Marmion" (c. 1760) near Fredericksburg, Virginia, has been installed at the Metropolitan Museum of Art, New York.

9. Farish, p. 95.

5. The Philadelphia Rococo, pp. 28-31

1. Morrison H. Heckscher and Leslie Green Bowman, *American Rococo, 1750-1775, Elegance in Ornament* (New York and Los Angeles: The Metropolitan Museum of Art, Los Angeles County Museum of Art, 1992), p . 182 .

2. Joseph T. Butler, *American Furniture* (London: Triune Books, 1973), pp. 46-51.

3. The designs on these papers were painted on in England according to specifications sent by American clients. Original examples can be seen at the Metropolitan Museum of Art (Van Rensselaer Room, c. 1768) and at the Jeremiah Lee Mansion in Marblehead, Massachusetts, c. 1768.

4. Catherine Lynn, *Wallpaper in America* (New York: W. W. Norton and Co., 1980), p. 56.

5. A re-creation of this decorative color scheme can be seen in the Governor's Palace at Colonial Williamsburg.

6. Farmers' Formal, pp. 32-35

1. At least one prosperous New England farmhouse is known to have been designed with a long-room across its entire front for the use of the local Masonic lodge. This room, and its painted decorations, has been preserved in the Salem Towne House at Old Sturbridge Village, Sturbridge, Massachusetts.

2. For the most comprehensive discussion of American wall painting, see Nina Fletcher Little, *American Decorative Wall Painting 1700-1850* (New York: E. P. Dutton, 1989).

3. Little categorizes several groups and notes specific characteristics of each.

4. Little, pp. 83, 95.

5. Ibid., 83-96.

7. Designs for a New Republic, pp. 36-39

1. The term "Federal" is a typically American label, referring to the neoclassical style popular during the early years of the American republic.

2. Refer to William H. Pierson, Jr., *American Buildings and Their Architects, The Colonial and Neoclassical Styles* (New York: Anchor Press/ Doubleday, 1976). For a good overview of the furniture of this period, see Charles F. Montgomery, *American Furniture, The Federal Period* (New York: The Viking Press, 1966).

3. Popular Pompeiian colors include various bright greens, pinks, terra cottas, oranges, blues, and black.

4. Painted floors were common during the late eighteenth and early nineteenth centuries. Thomas Jefferson had at least two floors painted grass-green, a color suggested by Gilbert Stuart, the eminent portraitist. See Jack McLaughlin, *Jefferson and Monticello* (New York: Henry Holt and Company, 1988), p. 316.

8. The Nation's Architect, pp. 40-43

1. A good discussion of Latrobe the architect can be found in Pierson, pp. 343-372, 400-403.

2. Jack L. Lindsey, "An Early Latrobe Furniture Commission," *The Magazine Antiques* (January, 1991), 209-210.

3. Ibid., pp. 208-219.

4. The walls of the room were apparently papered with a plain cream-colored paper and then overpainted with a flat paint of the same color. Plain paper was often applied to hide cracks in the plaster. See Seale, p. 126.

5. Latrobe's drawings of this furniture are extant. See Seale, pp. 106-107.

6. Margaret Brown Klapthor, "Benjamin Latrobe and Dolley Madison Decorate the White House 1809-1811," *United States Museum Bulletin* 241, paper 49 (Washington, D.C. : Smithsonian Institution, 1965), 160.

7. Ibid., p. 160.

8. Ibid., p. 162.

9. Ibid., p. 164.

10. Though no record of the actual carpet design remains, the color, designs, and general style make it tempting to suggest that this carpet may have actually been the one Latrobe chose.

9. Pineapples, Starbursts, and Swags, pp. 44-47

1. Little, p. 99.

2. Ibid. Little notes that many of the same designs have been found over large regions, raising interesting questions about their dissemination.

3. Ibid.

4. Ibid., p. 104. The example by Moses Eaton is from a house in Athol, Massachusetts.

10. Outdoors/Indoors, pp. 48-51

1. Little, p. 124. One of the best known of all the New England scenic painters was Rufus Porter (1792-1884), who painted chiefly between 1825 and 1840. Little notes that some of Porter's work included tropical trees and volcanoes probably inspired by a voyage to the Pacific Northwest and Hawaii between 1817 and 1819. Of course these remote locations were as unfamiliar to most Americans at the time as the surface of Mars is to most Americans living today. Evidently, Porter was able to convince some of his clients to let him paint unfamiliar scenes upon their walls. This practice very much appealed to him, and in 1846 he wrote about wall painting in one of a series of articles for *Scientific America*. "In finishing up scenery," he wrote, "it is neither necessary nor expedient, in all cases, to imitate nature. There are a great variety of beautiful designs which are easily and quickly produced with the brush, and which excel nature itself in a picturesque brilliancy, and richly embellish the work, though not in perfect lamination of anything."

2. Ibid., p. 123. One particularly impressive paper called "Les Voyages du Captaine Cook" or "Les Sauvages

de la Mer du Pacifique" was a riot of detail and color, showing the palm trees and scenery of a land that most Americans would never see. Designed and printed between 1804 and 1806, this paper is known to have been viewed by Rufus Porter during a visit to a house in Augusta, Maine.

3. Lynn, pp. 193, 195, 204. Interestingly, the creators of scenic papers often took the same artistic license as scenic painters. Of one paper, Dufour's "Monuments of Paris," Lynn notes that the major Parisian buildings illustrated are seemingly lined up along the Seine with no regard for their actual settings—a sort of glossary of French architecture. Of the Zuber paper in the White House, Lynn notes that the landscape depicting Boston is one common in other Zuber papers depicting European cities.

4. Little, pp 124-125.

5. These kinds of carpets, some of which were of the variety called "Venetian," were used in country settings well into the late nineteenth century.

11. Home and Hearth, pp. 52-55

1. Elisabeth Donaghy Garrett, At Home, *The American Family, 1750-1870* (New York (Harry N. Abrams, 1990), pp. 95-98.

2. During the wintertime, when kitchens were the warmest rooms in houses, using and furnishing them as family sitting rooms was logical.

3. Garrett, p. 98.

12. The Greek Revival, pp. 56-59

1. Many of these urban residences can still be seen in Manhattan. One of the most notable is the Old Merchant House (c. 1835), now a museum at East 4th Street. Cushman's Row, on West 20th Street between Ninth and Tenth Avenues in Chelsea, is also notable.

2. Baize is traditionally a woolen cloth similar to that used to cover billiard tables. Traditionally, baize is dark green, although various shades of olive and even brown existed.

3. The growth of the machine-made wallpaper industry in America was responsible for making wallpaper readily available and affordable.

4. These popular block papers are currently reproduced by several firms.

13. The Gothic Revival, pp. 60-63

1. The importance of both Downing and Davis is well covered in Pierson, pp. 270-431.

2. This popular book was reprinted by Dover Publications, New York, in 1969.

3. In the same way that the library or study was often associated with the masculine householder, the boudoir or sitting room was generally the reserve of the lady of the house. During a period when the effective running of even a modest-sized household could involve as many as four or five servants, this room was often the center of operations from where the complex tasks of household management were overseen. In *The Architecture of Country Houses*, a room called the boudoir was included in several floor plans on the first floor of large country houses—clear indication that the room's use was neither strictly nor necessarily associated with the lady's bedroom. Of a small boudoir to the right of the front door in a rural Gothic-style villa, Downing wrote: "On the right is a pretty little boudoir, or ladies' morning room, which could be fitted up in a delicate and tasteful manner, with chintz furniture, the walls papered with chaste Gothic or Elizabethan patterns, or ornamented with small and appropriate pictures or prints."

4. Andrew Jackson Downing, *The Architecture of Country Houses* (New York: Dover Publications, 1969), pp. 322, 332, 339, 353.

5. Alexander Jackson Davis, who designed Lyndhurst, Tarrytown, New York, also designed much of its furniture. The house is now owned by the National Trust and is open to the public.

14. Rococo Meets Renaissance, pp. 64-67

1. Among the best extant examples are houses located on West 21st, 22nd, and 23rd Streets between Ninth and Tenth Avenues in New York City.

2. An excellent study of this house form is in Charles Lockwood, *Bricks and Brownstone, The New York Row House, 1783-1929* (New York: McGraw-Hill Book Company, 1972), pp. 124-225.

3. William Seale, *Recreating the Historic House Interior* (Nashville: American Association for State and Local History, 1979), pp. 150-151.

4. The most famous mid-nineteenth-century Rococo-Revival furniture is that designed and carved by New York cabinetmaker John Henry Belter. Like most fine and costly furniture, the majority of Belter's characteristically highly carved and curvilinear pieces were made of rosewood. Other well-known cabinet-

makers who worked in this style included the Meeks brothers of New York and Prudent Mallard of New Orelans. Among cabinetmakers working in the Renaissance-Revival style were George Hunzinger of New York, John Jelliff of Newark, New Jersey, and Kimbel and Cabus, whose rosewood cabinets are especially important.

5. In all likelihood, a glimpse of this room in 1875 or so would have shown a general redecoration, including the replacement of the white marble mantel with one of dark wood, the globed chandelier, the curtains and carpet, and the introduction of a color scheme of deeper blues, duller reds, and more somber golds. True to the spirit of eclecticism which dominated the end of the century, the amount of furniture and accessories would have been increased and characteristically unmatched. Though parlor sets might remain in vogue a little while longer, they would be augmented with pieces of wicker, heavily upholstered chairs, and collections of china, brass, and small tables.

15. The Renaissance Revival, pp. 68-71

1. Interior views of this magnificent house are in Arnold Lewis, et al. *The Opulent Interiors of the Gilded Age* (New York: Dover Publications, 1987), pp. 33-39.

2. Many wooden houses of this style were built in San Francisco and survived the earthquake and fire of 1906.

3. Before mid-century, the library as a separate room in a house was uncommon. While rooms for the storage of books existed in eighteenth-century America, they were restricted to the houses of the highest classes. *The Architecture of County Houses* (1850) gave rooms known as libraries prominent location and generous floor area, but only in dwellings of the largest size. In writing about the villa, which he considered the home of America's "most leisurely and educated class of citizens," Andrew Jackson Downing wrote emphatically about the importance of devoting substantial space to the library or "cabinet sacred to books" as a most important feature of the inhabitant's "inner domestic life."

4. An excellent photograph of a Renaissance-Revival library, though grander than most, is that of the Stewart Mansion (now destroyed) in Lewis, p. 3.

16. The Exotic Craze, pp. 72-75

1. James West Davidson, et al., *Nation of Nations, A Narrative History of the American Republic* (New York: Alfred A. Knopf, 1991), pp. 642-681.

2. See Lewis.

3. Ibid., p. 117.

4. That the occupants of rooms like the Vanderbilt parlor would have been familiar with all the objects crowding their rooms is difficult to imagine.

5. The first important exhibition to take place in the United States was the great Philadelphia Centennial Exhibition of 1876.

6. There were few, if any, rooms decorated in one pure period or decorative style at this time.

17. Queen Anne in America, pp. 76-79

1. *The Gilded Age* (1874), by Mark Twain and Charles Dudley Warner, epitomizes the era.

2. Metcalf, pp. 173-174.

18. The First Colonial Revival, pp. 80-83

1. One of the best known is 28 Fayerweather Street, Cambridge, Massachusetts, designed by Sturgis and Brigham in 1882. Both its entrance piece and staircase detailing were copied from measured drawings of the Hancock House, demolished in 1863.

2. Apart from its Palladian window, one of the most imitated architectural motifs of Mount Vernon is its two-story colonade.

19. Bay Area Rustic/Classical, pp. 84-87

1. Richard Longstreth, *On the Edge of the World* (New York: The Architectural History Foundation, 1989), pp. 107-141.

2. Ibid., pp. 313-314.

3. Ibid., p. 315 ff.

4. Ibid., p. 107 ff.

5. Ibid., pp. 306-311.

20. Design Advice for the Elite, pp. 88-91

1. Alan Gowans, *Images of American Living* (Philadelphia: J. B. Lippincott Company, 1964), p. 366.

2. Architects included McKim, Mead and White, Richard Morris Hunt, Daniel Burnham, and Louis Sullivan.

3. For views of Wharton's rooms and of interiors designed by Codman, see Metcalf. For views of rooms

designed by de Wolfe, see Nina Campbell and Caroline Seebohm, *Elsie de Wolfe, A Decorative Life* (New York: Panache Press, Clarkson N. Potter, Inc., 1992).

21. Home Sweet Home, pp. 92-95

1. While the Sears, Roebuck catalog for 1897 was nearly 800 pages long and carried items from electric rings to ease rheumatism to fringe-topped surreys, many pages were dedicated to household items from shade pulls, towels, and bedding to furniture, chandeliers, and china. Every item was illustrated, down to the smallest paper clip, so it is not difficult to imagine how popular the catalog was with those—both young and old—who spent many idle hours browsing through its pages. A reprint of the 1897 catalog has been reproduced. See Fred L. Israel, ed., *1897 Sears, Roebuck Catalogue* (New York: Chelsea House Publishers, 1968).

23. The Craftsman Era, pp. 100-103

1. Folke Nyberg and Victor Steinbrueck, consultants, *An Urban Inventory for Seattle; Wallingford: An Inventory of Buildings and Urban Design Resources* (Seattle: Historic Seattle Preservation and Development Authority, 1975), "a note on the Wallingford Bungalow."

2. Frank Lloyd Wright, *The Natural House* (New York: The New American Library, 1954), p. 54.

3. Gustav Stickley, *The Best af Craftsman Homes* (Santa Barbara: Peregrine Smith, Inc., 1979), p. 205.

4. Ibid., p. 165.

5. Ibid., p. 89.

6. Ibid., p. 197.

24. The Spanish Revivals, pp. 104-107

1. As in Florida, the geographical setting, native plants, and climate were well-suited to the style.

2. See Shirley Johnston, *Palm Beach Houses* (New York: Rizzoli, 1991), for a lavish photographic survey of Florida houses in this style.

3. Middle-class houses in the style can be seen in Lawrence Grow, *The Old House Book of Cottages and Bungalows* (Pittstown, New Jersey: The Main Street Press, 1987), pp. 99-108.

4. Ibid.

25. Bankers' Tudor, pp. 108-111

1. See Grow, pp. 80-81 for two modest Tudor-Revival houses.

27. The International Style in America, pp. 116-119

1. This house is now owned and operated by the Society for the Preservation of New England Antiquities and is open to the public.

29. The Baby Boomer Era, pp. 124-127

1. A view of this room can be seen in Gerald W. R. Ward, "Three Centuries of Life along the Piscataqua River," *The Magazine Antiques* (July, 1992), p. 64.

30. Working It Out for Yourself, pp. 128-131

1. Downing, pp. 292-295.

Recommended Reading

Adams, William Howard. *Jefferson's Monticello*. New York: Abbeville Press, 1983.

Arts and Antiques, ed. *Nineteenth-Century Furniture: Innovation, Revival, and Reform*. New York: Billboard Publications, 1982.

Aslet, Clive. *The American Country House*. New Haven: Yale University Press, 1990.

Bayer, Patricia. *Art Deco Interiors, Decoration and Design Classics of the 1920s and 1930s*. A Bullfinch Press Book. Boston: Little, Brown and Company, 1990.

Blow, Michael, ed. *The American Heritage History of the Thirteen Colonies*. New York: American Heritage Publishing Co., 1967.

Boutelle, Sara Holmes. *Julia Morgan Architect*. New York: Abbeville Press, 1988.

Bunting, Bainbridge. *John Gaw Meem, Southwestern Architect*. Albuquerque: University of New Mexico Press, 1983.

Butler, Joseph T. *American Furniture*. London: Triune Books, 1973

Campbell, Nina and Caroline Seebohm. *Elsie de Wolfe, A Decorative Life*. New York: Panache Press, Clarkson N. Potter, 1992.

Cantor, Jay E. *Winterthur*. New York: Harry N. Abrams, 1986.

Cooke, Edward S., ed. *Upholstery in America and Europe from the Seventeenth Century to World War I*. New York: W. W. Norton & Co., 1987.

Cooper, Jeremy. *Victorian and Edwardian Decor*. New York: Abbeville Press, 1987.

Cummings, Abbott Lowell. *The Framed Houses of Massachusetts Bay, 1625-1725*. Cambridge: Harvard University Press, 1979.

Curtis, Nancy and Richard C. Nylander. *Beauport*. The Society for the Preservation of New England Antiquities. Boston: David R. Godine, 1990 .

Davidson, James West, et al. *Nation of Nations, A Narrative History of the American Republic*. New York: Alfred A. Knopf, 1991.

Davidson, Marshall B., ed. *The American Heritage History of Colonial Antiques*. New York: American Heritage Publishing Co., 1967.

Dowling, Elizabeth. *American Classicist, The Architecture of Philip Trammell Shutze*. New York: Rizzoli, 1989.

Downing, Andrew Jackson. *The Architecture of Country Houses*. Repr. New York: Dover Publications, 1969.

Downing, Antoinette F. and Vincent J. Scully, Jr. *The Architectural Heritage of Newport, Rhode Island, 1640-1915*. New York: Bramhall House, 1967.

Duncan, Alastair. *American Art Deco*. New York: Harry N. Abrams, 1986.

Durant, Stuart. *Ornament, From the Industrial Revolution to Today*. New York: The Overlook Press, 1986.

Eastlake, Charles L. *Hints on Household Taste*. Repr. New York: Dover Publications, 1978.

Farish, Hunter Dickinson, ed. *The Journal and Letters of Philip Vickers Fithian, 1773-1774*. Williamsburg: Colonial Williamsburg, 1965.

Fitch, James Marston. *Walter Gropius*. New York: George Braziller, 1960.

Flynt, William A. and Joseph Peter Spang. "Exterior Architectural Embellishment." *The Magazine Antiques* (March, 1985), 632-639.

Foreman, John and Robbe Pierce Stimson. *The Vanderbilts and the Gilded Age*. New York: St. Martin's Press, 1991.

Frangiamore, Catherine Lynn. *Wallpapers in Historic Preservation*. Washington, D.C.: National Park Service, 1977.

Garrett, Elisabeth Donaghy. *At Home, The American Family 1750-1870*. New York: Harry N. Abrams, 1990.

Gowans, Alan. *Images of American Living*. Philadelphia: J. B. Lippincott Co., 1964.

Greif, Martin. *Depression Modern: The Thirties Style in America*. New York: Universe Books, 1975.

Grow, Lawrence. *The Old House Book of Cottages and Bungalows*. Pittstown, N.J.: The Main Street Press, 1987.

——————— and Dina Von Zweck. *American Victorian*. New York: Harper & Row, 1984.

Hampton, Mark. *Legendary Decorators of the Twentieth Century*. New York: Doubleday, 1992.

Harris, Nathaniel. *Chippendale*. New Jersey: Chartwell Books, 1989.

Heckscher, Morrison H. and Leslie Greene Bowman. *American Rococo, 1750-1775: Elegance in Ornament*. The Metropolitan Museum of Art and The Los Angeles County Museum of Art. New York: Harry N. Abrams, 1992.

Hewitt, Mark Alan. *The Architect and the American Country House.* New Haven: Yale University Press, 1990.

——————————. *The Architecture of Mott B. Schmidt.* New York: Rizzoli, 1991.

Israel, Fred L., ed. *1987 Sears, Roebuck Catalogue.* New York: Chelsea House Publishers, 1968.

Johnston, Shirley. *Palm Beach Houses.* New York: Rizzoli, 1991.

Jordy, William H. *American Buildings and Their Architects, The Impact of European Modernism in the Mid-Twentieth Century.* New York: Anchor Books, 1976.

Klapthor, Margaret Brown. "Benjamin Latrobe and Dolley Madison Decorate the White House 1809-1811." *United States National Museum Bulletin* 241, paper 49 (1965), Smithsonian Instututution, 153-164.

Lancaster, Clay. *The American Bungalow 1880-1930.* New York: Abbeville Press, 1985.

Lewis, Arnold, et al. *The Opulent Interiors of the Gilded Age.* New York: Dover Publications, 1987.

Lindsey, Jack L. "An Early Latrobe Furniture Commission." *The Magazine Antiques* (January, 1991), 208-219.

Little, Nina Fletcher. *American Decorative Wall Painting 1700-1850.* New York: E. P. Dutton, 1989.

Lockwood, Charles. *Bricks and Brownstone, The New York Row House, 1783-1920, An Architectural History.* New York: McGraw-Hill, 1972.

Longstreth, Richard. *On the Edge of the World.* The Architectural History Foundation. Cambridge, Mass.: The MIT Press, 1983.

Lynn, Catherine. *Wallpaper in America, From the Seventeenth Century to World War I.* New York: W. W. Norton & Co., 1980.

Mayhew, Edgar deN. and Minor Myers, Jr. *A Documentary History of American Interiors from the Colonial Era to 1915.* New York: Charles Scribner's Sons, 1980.

McCorquodale, Charles. *The History of Interior Decoration.* Oxford: Phaidon Press, 1983.

McLaughlin, Jack. *Jefferson and Monticello, The Biograhpy of a Builder.* New York: Henry Holt Company, 1988.

Metcalf, Pauline C., ed. *Ogden Codman and the Decoration of Houses.* Boston: The Boston Athenaeum, 1988.

The Metropolitan Museum of Art. *In Pursuit of Beauty: Americans and the Aesthetic Movement.* New York: Rizzoli, 1986.

Miller, R. Craig. *Modern Design 1890-1990 in the Metropolitan Museum of Art.* New York: Harry N. Abrams, 1990.

Montgomery, Charles F. *American Furniture, The Federal Period in the Henry Francis du Pont Winterthur Museum.* New York: The Viking Press, 1966.

Montgomery, Florence M. *Textiles in America, 1650-1870.* New York: W. W. Norton & Co., 1984.

Mosca, Matthew John. "The House [Mount Vernon] and Its Restoration." *The Magazine Antiques* (February, 1989), 462-473.

Moss, Roger W. *Lighting for Historic Buildings.* Washington, D.C.: The Preservation Press, 1988.

Nyberg, Folke and Victor Steinbrueck, eds. *A Visual Inventory of Buildings and Urban Resources for Seattle, Washington.* Seattle: Historic Seattle Preservation and Development Authority, 1975.

Nylander, Jane C. *Fabrics for Historic Buildings.* Washington, D.C.: The Preservation Press, 1983.

Nylander, Richard C. *Wallpapers for Historic Buildings.* Washington, D.C.: The Preservation Press, 1983.

Penn, Theodore Zuk. "Decorative and Protective Finishes, 1750-1850, Materials, Process, and Craft." *The Bulletin for the Association for Preservation Technology,* vol. XVI, no. 1 (1984), 3-45.

Pierson, William H., Jr. *American Buildings and Their Architects. The Colonial and Neo-Classical Styles.* Garden City, N.Y.: Anchor Books, 1976.

——————————. *American Buildings and Their Architects: Technology and the Picturesque.* New York: Doubleday and Co., 1978.

Poppeliers, John C., et al. *What Style Is It?* Washington, D.C.: The Preservation Press, 1983.

Ramsey, Charles G. and Harold R. Sleeper. *Architectural Graphic Standards.* New York: John Wiley and Sons, 1970.

Reynolds, Hezekiah. *Directions for House and Ship Painting.* Repr. of 1812 ed. Worcester, Mass.: American Antiquarian Society, 1978.

Rodgers, Dorothy. *The House in My Head.* New York: Atheneum, 1967.

Schoeser, Mary and Celia Rufey. *English and American Textiles from 1790 to the Present.* New York: Thames and Hudson, 1989.

Schwin, Lawrence, III. *Old House Colors.* New York: Sterling Publishing Co., 1990.

Scully, Vincent J., Jr. *The Shingle Style and the Stick Style: Architectural Theory and Design from Downing to the Origins of Wright.* New Haven: Yale University Press, 1973.

Seale, William. *The President's House, A History.* Washington, D.C.: White House Historical Association, 1986.

——————— . *Recreating the Historic House Interior.* Nashville, Tenn.: American Association for State and Local History, 1979.

———————.*The Tasteful Interlude: American Interiors through the Camera's Eye, 1860-1917.* New York: Praeger Publishers, 1975.

Sears, Roebuck and Co. *Sears, Roebuck Home Builder's Catalogue: The Complete Illustrated l910 Edition.* New York: Dover Publications, 1990.

Slavin, Richard E., III. *Opulent Textiles.* New York: Crown Publishers, 1992.

Stayton, Kevin L. *Dutch by Design The Schenck Houses at the Brooklyn Museum.* New York: The Brooklyn Museum in association with Phaidon Universe, 1990.

Stickley, Gustav. *The Best of Craftsman Homes.* Santa Barbara: Peregrine Smith, Inc., 1979.

Stillinger, Elizabeth. *Historic Deerfield.* New York: Dutton Studio Books/Penguin, 1992.

Taylor, Anne. *Southwestern Ornamentation and Design.* Santa Fe: Sunstone Press, 1989.

Taylor, Lonn and Dessa Bokides. *New Mexican Furniture 1600-1940.* Santa Fe: Museum of New Mexico Press, 1987.

Thornton, Peter. *Authentic Decor: The Domestic Interior 1620-1920.* New York: Viking Penguin, 1984.

Van Doren, Carl. *Benjamin Franklin.* New York: The Viking Press, 1938.

Ward, Gerald W. R. "Three Centuries of Life along the Piscataqua River." *The Magazine Antiques* (July, 1992), 60-66.

Wharton, Edith and Ogden Codman, Jr. *The Decoration of Houses.* Repr. New York: W. W. Norton & Co., 1978.

Winkler, Gail Caskey and Roger W. Moss. *Victorian Interior Decoration, American Interiors 1830-1900.* New York: Henry Holt & Co., 1986.

Wilhide, Elizabeth. *William Morris Decor and Design.* New York: Harry N. Abrams, 1991.

Wright, Frank Lloyd. *The Natural House.* New York: The New American Library, 1954.

Acknowledgments

MANY PEOPLE have helped in the creation of this book and are owed my heartfelt thanks, particularly for their generous assistance born of a genuine interest in the project.

Several people at Sterling Publishing Company in New York deserve special thanks, not only for their warm enthusiasm but for their help in solving many difficult technical problems. These include Charles Nurnberg, John Woodside, Jean Engel, Emma Gonzalez, and of course Karen Nelson who designed the cover. Among his other responsibilities, my editor, Martin Greif, has been my liaison with the outside world for the past two years.

Gathering the textile, wallpaper, and carpet samples, and the other objects that appear throughout the book, proved to be a time-consuming task, but one made easier and enjoyable for the many people who graciously offered their knowledge and help. Several have become friends, which is an added dividend. First, grateful thanks to Dave Ryan, who made many of the initial contacts and gathered countless samples. Thanks, too, to Bruce Bradbury, Paul Duscherer, and Therese Tierney of Bradbury and Bradbury Art Wallpapers; Murray B. Douglas and Judy Straeter of Brunschwig & Fils, Inc.; John R. Burrows of J. R. Burrows and Company, Historical Design Merchants and Woodward Grosvenor & Co., Ltd.; Christopher S. Hyland of Christopher Hyland, Inc.; John Buscemi of Classic Revivals, Inc.; Gail K. Burger and Kenneth Kipps of The Colonial Williamsburg Foundation; Marcia Gagliardi of Haley's Antiques, Athol, Massachusetts, and Robert B. Mayer; Ted Curtin of Heart of the Wood; Carol Mead of Carol Mead; Robert and Argine Carter of Mt. Diablo Handprints; Mark Saley of Old World Weavers, a division of Stark Carpet Corporation; Ed Pinson and Debrah Ware of PY-WE-ACK Studio; Michael Stiles, Alan Ransome, and Randy Van Syoc of Michael Stiles and Toad Hall; Ed and Kathleen B. Smith of Textile Reproductions; Rabbit Goody and Stanley Horton, Jr., of Thistle Hill Weavers; Marie Montera, Nancy Picunko, and William H. Wagner, President, of Arthur Sanderson and Sons; Robert F. S. Bitter, Maryelisabeth Chomas, Dr. Frank Koe, and Leslie Desgeorges of Scalamandré; Marjorie McNaughton, Don Roberts, Camille Madonna, Richard B. Slavin III, and J. P. Hayden, Jr., of F. Schumacher & Co.; and Patricia Siskin and Bonnie Sonnenschein of Stroheim and Romann, Inc. Special thanks are also due to William Seale, who suggested including the chapter on Latrobe and the Madisons' Oval Salon, and to Betty Monkman, assistant curator at The White House, who suggested research materials. Thanks also to Guy Evans Ltd., Richard Humphries of the Humphries Weaving Company, and Kate Smith of Eaton Hill Textile Works.

I owe a particular debt to friends and family, many of whom adjusted their lives to accommodate the project and understood my need to work and research. These include my colleagues Herb Githens and John Terrerri, who reviewed the information on pages 138 through 143, Mary Evelyn and Bob Miner, Eleanor and Steve Orlando, Josephine Bartell, Delna and Bob Stefanow, and Joan, Allen, Larry, and Lois Maples. I offer thanks, too, to my aunt, Elsie Binder, who encouraged my early interest in drawing.

Finally, I acknowledge a special debt to Ed Connolly, who assisted in typing the manuscript and went beyond the call of friendship in many ways to help me through the complexities of the book. His aid in assisting my mother, Lois, to conquer the word processor was of great help, as was her typing of the manuscript and execution of many administrative details necessary throughout the project. I am grateful to her for providing me with the considerable office space needed to write and design the book. Her encouragement has always been freely given and deeply appreciated.

Photographic Credits

Except as noted below, all photographs in this book were taken by the author, who wishes to thank those companies and private individuals who provided fabrics, wallpapers, carpets, and decorative objects. All of the books, engravings, and period photographs shown are from the author's collection, as are the wall elevations from H. D. & J. Moeller and the fabrics and carpet shown on pages 46 (1), 95, 99 (5), 114 (2), 122 (2), and 126 (2 and 6).

The following photographs were provided by the companies and individuals listed below and are used with their permission:

- Bradbury and Bradbury Art Wallpapers, pages 74 (1), 110 (5).
- Brunschwig & Fils, Inc., page 30.
- Classic Revivals, Inc., pages 15, 22, 46, 58, 62.
- Heart of the Wood, pages 14, 110, 111.

- PY-WE-ACK Studio, pages 102, 103.

- F. Schumacher & Co., pages 19, 27, 62, 90, 110 (3), 111 (6), 114, 115, 118, 119.

- Michael Stiles and Toad Hall, page 51.

- Woodward Grosvenor & Co., Ltd. and J. R. Burrows and Company, pages 38, 39, 43, 59, 62, 66 (2, 3, and 4), 70 (1, 2, 4, 5, and 6), 78, 82, 87, 103.

- Herbert J. Githens, Architect, plans on pages 139 and 140.

Index